The Essential HVAC

[12 in 1] Master HVAC Systems in No Time – From Basics to Expert-Level Installation, Maintenance, and Troubleshooting for Energy- Efficient, Healthy Homes and Workplaces

Author

Paul Main

© Copyright 2024 Paul Main

All Rights Reserved.

Protected with: www.protectmywork.com.

This document provides exact and reliable information regarding the topic and issues covered.

In no way is it legal to reproduce, duplicate, or transmit any part of this document in either electronic means or in printed format. All rights reserved.

The information provided in this book is stated to be truthful and consistent. Any liability, in terms of inattention or otherwise, by any usage or abuse of any policies, processes, or directions contained within is the sole responsibility of the recipient reader. Under no circumstances will any legal responsibility or blame be held against the publisher for any reparation, damages, or monetary loss due to the information herein, either directly or indirectly.

Respective authors own all copyrights not held by the publisher.

The information in this book is solely offered for informational purposes and is universal. The presentation of the information is without a contract or any guaranteed assurance.

The trademarks used are without any consent, and the trademark publication is without permission or backing by the trademark owner. All trademarks and brands within this book are for clarifying purposes only and are owned by the owners, not affiliated with this document.

TABLE CONTENT

INTRODUCTION 7
BOOK 1 9
HVAC BASICS AND CORE CONCEPTS 9
CHAPTER 1: OVERVIEW OF HVAC SYSTEMS..10
CHAPTER 2: DIFFERENT TYPES OF HVAC SYSTEMS..12
CHAPTER 3: KEY TERMINOLOGY 15
CHAPTER 4: SAFETY GUIDELINES 17
CHAPTER 5: BASIC PRINCIPLES 19
BOOK 2 21
DETAILED HVAC COMPONENTS 21
CHAPTER 6: HEATING SOLUTIONS..22
CHAPTER 7: VENTILATION SYSTEMS 25
CHAPTER 8: COOLING SYSTEMS 28
CHAPTER 9: CONTROLS AND THERMOSTATS 32
BOOK 3 36
TECHNIQUES FOR HVAC INSTALLATION 36
CHAPTER 10: PRE-INSTALLATION PLANNING 37
CHAPTER 11: HEATING SYSTEM INSTALLATION 39
CHAPTER 12: AIR CONDITIONING INSTALLATION 43
CHAPTER 13: VENTILATION SYSTEM INSTALLATION 47
BOOK 4 50
HVAC MAINTENANCE AND PROBLEM-SOLVING 50
CHAPTER 14: ROUTINE MAINTENANCE TASKS 51
CHAPTER 15: IDENTIFYING COMMON HVAC PROBLEMS 53
CHAPTER 16: TROUBLESHOOTING METHODS 56
CHAPTER 17: PROFESSIONAL MAINTENANCE SERVICES 59
BOOK 5 62
ESSENTIAL HVAC TOOLS AND EQUIPMENT 62
CHAPTER 18: BASIC HVAC TOOLS..63
CHAPTER 19: ADVANCED HVAC TOOLS 66

- CHAPTER 20: MAINTAINING YOUR TOOLS 68
- CHAPTER 21: SAFETY EQUIPMENT 71
- BOOK 6: 74
- DESIGNING AND PLANNING HVAC SYSTEMS 74
- CHAPTER 22: CALCULATING LOADS 75
- CHAPTER 23: DESIGNING DUCTWORK 78
- CHAPTER 24: IMPLEMENTING SYSTEM ZONING 81
- CHAPTER 25: ENHANCING ENERGY EFFICIENCY 84
- CHAPTER 26: INSULATION AND SEALING 87
- BOOK 7: 90
- ADVANCED HVAC SYSTEMS AND TECHNOLOGIES 90
- CHAPTER 27: VARIABLE REFRIGERANT FLOW (VRF) SYSTEMS 91
- CHAPTER 28: GEOTHERMAL HEAT PUMPS 95
- CHAPTER 29: HYDRONIC HEATING SYSTEMS 99
- CHAPTER 30: SMART HVAC SOLUTIONS 102
- CHAPTER 31: DUCTLESS HVAC SYSTEMS 105
- BOOK 8: 108
- HVAC REGULATIONS, STANDARDS, AND BUSINESS GUIDE 108
- CHAPTER 32: UNDERSTANDING BUILDING CODES 109
- CHAPTER 33: SAFETY STANDARDS IN HVAC 113
- CHAPTER 34: ENVIRONMENTAL REGULATIONS 117
- CHAPTER 35: HVAC CERTIFICATION AND LICENSING 121
- CHAPTER 36: STARTING AND RUNNING AN HVAC BUSINESS 125
- BOOK 9: 129
- SPECIALIZED HVAC APPLICATIONS AND INDOOR AIR QUALITY 129
- CHAPTER 37: ADAPTING HVAC FOR DIFFERENT CLIMATES 130
- CHAPTER 38: INDOOR AIR QUALITY (IAQ) MANAGEMENT 134
- CHAPTER 39: HVAC IN SPECIALIZED SETTINGS 137
- BOOK 10: 140
- THE FUTURE OF HVAC AND REAL-WORLD CASE STUDIES 140
- CHAPTER 40: INNOVATIONS AND EMERGING TECHNOLOGIES 141

CHAPTER 41: SUSTAINABLE HVAC PRACTICES 145

CHAPTER 42: TRENDS AND FUTURE DIRECTIONS 149

CHAPTER 43: RETROFITTING AND UPGRADING HVAC SYSTEMS 153

CHAPTER 44: SOFTWARE TOOLS AND CASE STUDIES 156

BOOK 11: 161

SMART HOME INTEGRATION WITH HVAC 161

CHAPTER 45: OVERVIEW OF SMART HOME SYSTEMS 162

CHAPTER 46: POPULAR SMART THERMOSTATS 165

CHAPTER 47: VOICE CONTROL INTEGRATION 168

CHAPTER 48: THERMAL ENERGY STORAGE IN SMART HVAC SYSTEMS 171

CHAPTER 49: TROUBLESHOOTING SMART HVAC SYSTEMS 174

BOOK 12: 177

THE ROLE OF HVAC IN HEALTH AND WELLNESS 177

CHAPTER 50: AIR QUALITY AND ITS IMPACT ON HEALTH 178

CHAPTER 51: HVAC SYSTEMS AND SLEEP QUALITY 180

CHAPTER 52: REDUCING VIRUS SPREAD WITH HVAC 183

CHAPTER 53: MENTAL HEALTH AND INDOOR COMFORT 186

CHAPTER 54: HUMIDITY CONTROL FOR WELLNESS 189

CONCLUSION 192

Preface

Welcome to "The Essential HVAC Handbook," your comprehensive guide to mastering heating, ventilation, and air conditioning systems. This book is meticulously crafted to serve as both a beginner's tutorial and an advanced practitioner's reference. It incorporates insights from industry experts and is meticulously updated to reflect the latest advancements and best practices in the field. Our goal is to empower you with the knowledge and skills necessary to understand, troubleshoot, and optimize HVAC systems effectively.

How to Use This Guide

Designed with the reader in mind, this guide is organized to facilitate easy learning and application. Each chapter is structured to progressively introduce you to HVAC concepts, starting from basic principles and gradually moving to more complex installations and troubleshooting techniques. Here's how to make the most out of this guide:

Structured Learning: Follow the chapters in sequence to build your knowledge base systematically.

Practical Application: Engage with step-by-step guides and practical examples that simulate real-world scenarios.

Whether you dip into specific sections as a reference or read through sequentially for a comprehensive understanding, this guide aims to be flexible and accommodating to your needs.

About the Author

Paul Main the author of this guide, brings over twenty years of field experience in HVAC systems, covering both the academic aspects of teaching and practical, hands-on applications. Having worked on numerous residential and commercial projects Paul Main offers a unique perspective that blends deep technical knowledge with real-world pragmatism, making this book an invaluable resource for anyone serious about HVAC.

Introduction

Welcome to the comprehensive guide that will take you through the entire spectrum of HVAC (Heating, Ventilation, and Air Conditioning) knowledge, from the foundational basics to the most advanced technologies. This book is designed to be your go-to resource, whether you're just starting or looking to deepen your expertise.

Why This Book Matters:

HVAC systems are critical to maintaining comfort, safety, and efficiency in both residential and commercial environments. Understanding these systems in-depth is essential for professionals in the field, homeowners looking to optimize their systems, and anyone interested in the latest advancements in technology.

What to Expect:

Our book is structured into ten detailed sections, each focusing on different aspects of HVAC systems. Here's a brief overview of what you'll learn:

1. Basics and Core Concepts: Begin with an introduction to HVAC systems, including definitions, key components, and the evolution of technology. Understand the basic system configurations and the future trends shaping the industry.

2. Detailed HVAC Components: Dive into the specifics of heating solutions, ventilation systems, cooling systems, and controls. Explore the various components that make up these systems and how they function together.

3. Techniques for HVAC Installation: Learn the essential techniques for planning, installing, and troubleshooting HVAC systems. This section covers everything from pre-installation planning to the installation processes for different types of systems.

4. HVAC Maintenance and Problem-Solving: Discover the best practices for routine maintenance, identifying common problems, and advanced troubleshooting methods. Understand how to keep your HVAC systems running smoothly and efficiently.

5. Essential HVAC Tools and Equipment: Get acquainted with the tools and equipment necessary for HVAC work, from basic hand tools to advanced diagnostic instruments. Learn how to maintain and select the right tools for various tasks.

6. Designing and Planning HVAC Systems: Explore the principles of designing HVAC systems, including load calculations, ductwork design, and system zoning. Learn how to plan effective HVAC solutions tailored to different needs.

7. Advanced HVAC Systems and Technologies: Delve into cutting-edge technologies such as Variable Refrigerant Flow (VRF) systems, geothermal heat pumps, and smart HVAC solutions. Understand the latest advancements and their applications.

8. HVAC Regulations, Standards, and Business Guide: Gain insights into building codes, safety standards, environmental regulations, and business practices related to HVAC. Learn about certification, licensing, and running a successful HVAC business.

9. Specialized HVAC Applications and Indoor Air Quality: Examine HVAC systems tailored for specialized settings like commercial, industrial, and healthcare environments. Focus on indoor air quality management and adapting HVAC systems to various climates.

10. The Futuåre of HVAC and Real-World Case Studies: Look ahead at emerging trends and innovations in HVAC technology. Explore case studies that showcase real-world applications and success stories, providing practical insights into the future of the industry.

Why This Book is Unique:

Our approach combines detailed technical information with practical applications, real-world case studies, and forward-looking insights. We aim to make complex concepts accessible and engaging, helping you build a solid understanding of HVAC systems and stay ahead in a rapidly evolving field.

Getting Started:

Each chapter is crafted to provide clear explanations, practical advice, and hands-on tips. We invite you to explore the chapters at your own pace, diving into topics that interest you and building your knowledge step-by-step.

Thank you for choosing this comprehensive guide to HVAC systems. We hope this book will be a valuable resource on your journey through the world of HVAC.

Fundamentals of HVAC

Understanding the fundamentals of HVAC is crucial whether you're starting your journey or refreshing your knowledge. This initial section introduces you to the core concepts that are the building blocks of all HVAC systems. Topics covered include:

Thermodynamics Basics: How energy is transferred within HVAC systems.

System Components: Detailed overview of components like compressors, fans, ducts, and controls.

System Types: Exploration of various types of HVAC systems, such as split systems, packaged units, and hybrids, and their applications.

Regulations and Standards: An overview of the regulatory framework governing HVAC installation and maintenance.

Book 1

HVAC Basics and Core Concepts

Chapter 1: Overview of HVAC Systems

Definition and Importance

Heating, Ventilation, and Air Conditioning (HVAC) systems are crucial for creating comfortable indoor environments. They control temperature, humidity, and air quality to optimize comfort and health. Given their vital role in residential, commercial, and industrial settings, understanding HVAC systems is essential not only for professionals in the field but also for property owners and managers.

Key Components

At the heart of every HVAC system are several key components that ensure its efficient operation:

Thermostat: The user interface that regulates the system's settings according to the desired temperature.

Air Handlers and Furnaces: These units circulate air throughout the building, with furnaces generating heat when needed.

Condensing Units: Typically located outside, these units release or collect heat from the air, depending on the mode.

Vents and Ducts: Pathways that deliver conditioned air to different areas and return it to the system for reconditioning.

Filters and Humidifiers: These components improve air quality by removing contaminants and controlling humidity.

Evolution of HVAC Technology

The history of HVAC technology is marked by advancements that have increased efficiency and environmental sustainability. Innovations include:

Automated Controls: Advanced thermostats and building management systems for better energy management.

Green Technologies: Systems designed for greater energy efficiency and reduced environmental impact, such as geothermal heating and cooling.

Smart Systems: HVAC units integrated with IoT technology, allowing remote monitoring and management.

Typical Applications

HVAC systems find applications across various domains:

Residential: Enhancing home comfort and energy efficiency.

Commercial: Essential for businesses, hospitals, schools, and retail spaces to ensure a comfortable, healthy environment for occupants.

Industrial: Used in manufacturing and warehousing to protect products and maintain safe working conditions.

Advantages and Disadvantages

While HVAC systems offer numerous benefits, they also present challenges:

Advantages: Increased comfort, improved air quality, enhanced energy efficiency, and greater control over indoor environments.

Disadvantages: High installation and maintenance costs, significant energy consumption, and potential environmental impact from certain refrigerants and energy sources.

Basic System Configurations

Understanding various HVAC configurations helps in selecting the right system for specific needs:

Split Systems: Comprising separate indoor and outdoor units, these are common in residential settings.

Packaged Systems: All components are housed in one unit, which is typically placed outside, making it ideal for small commercial buildings.

Hybrid Systems: These combine elements of both traditional and modern systems to optimize energy use and performance.

Future Trends in HVAC

The future of HVAC is focused on innovation and sustainability:

Integration of Renewable Energy: Increasing use of solar and wind energy to power HVAC systems.

Enhanced Automation and Smart Controls: Further developments in smart technologies for improved system efficiency and user control.

Sustainability Practices: Emphasis on reducing carbon footprints and enhancing system recyclable.

Chapter 2: Different Types of HVAC Systems

Residential vs. Commercial Systems

Residential Systems:
Residential HVAC systems are designed to provide comfort in homes and small apartments. They typically feature simpler setups with single-zone control systems. Common residential systems include:
Split Systems: Consisting of an indoor air handler and an outdoor condenser, ideal for cooling or heating individual rooms.
Packaged Units: All components are housed in a single unit, often installed outside the home, which is space-efficient for smaller properties.

Commercial Systems:
Commercial HVAC systems are more complex, and designed to handle larger spaces such as office buildings, shopping centers, and hospitals. They often include:
Centralized Systems: A large unit or multiple interconnected units that manage the climate of the entire building, providing consistent temperature control.
Variable Air Volume (VAV) Systems: Allow different areas of a building to have customized temperatures, enhancing energy efficiency and comfort.

Centralized vs. Decentralized Units

Centralized Units:
Centralized HVAC systems use one main unit to control the climate of an entire building or large area. These systems typically involve:
Chillers and Boilers: Centralized cooling and heating sources that distribute conditioned air through extensive ductwork.
Advantages: Efficient for large buildings, consistent temperature control, and ease of maintenance in one location.
Disadvantages: High initial installation cost and potentially higher energy consumption if not properly managed.

Decentralized Units:
Decentralized systems consist of multiple smaller units, each serving a specific zone or room. Examples include:
Window Air Conditioners: Ideal for single rooms or small areas.
Mini Split Systems: Provide heating and cooling to individual rooms or zones without extensive duct work.
Advantages: Lower initial cost, easy to install, and flexible for modifying temperature settings in different areas.
Disadvantages: May have higher operating costs and less uniform temperature distribution.

Split and Packaged Systems

Split Systems:

Split systems are the most common type for residential and small commercial applications. They include:

Indoor Unit: Contains the evaporator coil and air handler.

Outdoor Unit: Houses the condenser and compressor.

Advantages: Energy efficient, quieter operation, and flexible installation.

Disadvantages: Requires ductwork, which can be cumbersome to install in existing buildings.

Packaged Systems:

Packaged systems have all components housed in a single unit, often placed on the roof or ground. These systems include:

All-in-One Unit: Combines heating, cooling, and sometimes even air handling in a single package.

Advantages: Space-saving, easy to install, and ideal for buildings without existing ductwork.

Disadvantages: Limited to certain sizes and capacities, and might not be as efficient for large buildings.

Hybrid Systems

Hybrid HVAC systems integrate traditional heating and cooling methods with alternative energy sources. Examples include:

Heat Pump Systems: Combine electric heat pumps with a traditional furnace for more efficient heating and cooling.

Advantages: Improved energy efficiency, reduced reliance on fossil fuels, and cost savings over time.

Disadvantages: Higher upfront costs and potential complexity in system management.

Ductless Systems

Ductless HVAC systems, also known as mini-split systems, offer a flexible solution for heating and cooling without the need for ductwork. Features include:

Indoor Units: Mounted on walls or ceilings in each room.

Outdoor Unit: Connects to the indoor units via refrigerant lines.

Advantages: Easy installation, energy efficient, and ideal for retrofitting buildings without existing ducts.

Disadvantages: Higher initial cost per unit and visible indoor components.

Zoned HVAC Systems

Zoned HVAC systems allow for the independent control of temperatures in different areas or rooms of a building. They can be achieved through:

Multiple Thermostats: Each zone has its thermostat, controlling the HVAC unit for that specific area.

Motorized Dampers: Installed in the ductwork to regulate airflow to different zones.

Advantages: Increased comfort, energy savings by heating or cooling only occupied zones, and enhanced control.
Disadvantages: Higher installation complexity and cost.

Comparative Analysis

When comparing different HVAC systems, consider the following factors:

Cost: Initial installation, maintenance, and operating costs can vary widely between system types.

Efficiency: Look at SEER (Seasonal Energy Efficiency Ratio) ratings and other efficiency metrics to evaluate performance.

Comfort Control: Systems with advanced zoning and variable settings offer better control over indoor climates.

Space Requirements: Ductless and packaged systems may be preferable for spaces with limited installation options.

Environmental Impact: Consider systems that utilize renewable energy sources or have lower emissions.

Chapter 3: Key Terminology

Common Industry Terms
Airflow: The movement of air within a space, which is crucial for maintaining indoor air quality and comfort.
Heat Load: The amount of heat energy that must be removed from a space to maintain a desired temperature.
SEER (Seasonal Energy Efficiency Ratio): A measure of air conditioning and heat pump cooling efficiency, which indicates the amount of energy needed to provide a specific cooling output.

Specific Jargon
Plenum: A space or chamber in an HVAC system that can serve as a distribution area for heating or cooling air. There are typically two types: supply plenum and return plenum.
Refrigerant: A chemical compound used in HVAC systems to absorb and release heat as it transitions between liquid and gaseous states.
Ductwork: The system of ducts used to transport air from the HVAC unit to the various rooms of a building.

Units and Symbols
°F (Fahrenheit) and °C (Celsius): The units of measurement for temperature.
BTU (British Thermal Unit): A unit of heat; it is the amount of heat required to raise the temperature of one pound of water by one degree Fahrenheit.
CFM (Cubic Feet per Minute): A measure of airflow volume, indicating how much air can move in one minute.

Acronyms and Abbreviations
HVAC: Heating, Ventilation, and Air Conditioning.
AHU: Air Handling Unit, a device used to condition and circulate air as part of an HVAC system.
HSPF (Heating Seasonal Performance Factor): A measure used to gauge the efficiency of a heat pump.

Glossary of Essential Terms
Condenser Coil: Located in the outdoor unit, it releases the heat removed from the air by expelling it outside the building.
Evaporator Coil: Located in the indoor unit, it absorbs heat from the air inside your home, cooling it.
Thermostat: A device that monitors and regulates the temperature of a space by controlling the operation of an HVAC system.

Usage in Context

Each term has a specific usage in HVAC practice. For instance:

When discussing energy efficiency, one might say, "This system has a SEER rating of 16, which means it's highly efficient compared to older models with SEER "

In installation, a technician might note, "Ensure the CFM settings align with the size of the room to optimize airflow and energy consumption."

Technical Specifications

Understanding technical specifications is key for selecting, installing, and maintaining HVAC systems. Specifications might include:

Capacity: Often measured in tons, it indicates the amount of heat an HVAC system can remove from a home in one hour.

Energy Consumption: Typically listed in kilowatts (kW), this specifies how much power an HVAC unit uses during operation.

Noise Level: Measured in decibels (dB), it indicates how loud an HVAC system will be when running.

Chapter 4: Safety Guidelines

General Safety Practices

Safety is paramount in the HVAC industry due to the potential hazards associated with installation, maintenance, and repair work. Here are some general safety practices:

Follow Protocols: Always adhere to established safety protocols and procedures.

Work Area: Keep your work area clean and free of hazards. Ensure that tools and materials are properly stored and that walkways are unobstructed.

Training: Ensure all personnel are properly trained and certified for the tasks they are performing.

Communication: Maintain clear communication with team members to avoid accidents and ensure everyone is aware of their responsibilities and potential hazards.

Tool and Equipment Safety

Proper use and maintenance of tools and equipment are crucial for preventing accidents and ensuring efficiency:

Inspection: Regularly inspect tools and equipment for damage or wear. Replace or repair any defective items immediately.

Usage: Use tools and equipment only for their intended purpose. Follow the manufacturer's instructions for safe operation.

Storage: Store tools and equipment in designated areas when not in use to prevent tripping hazards and damage.

Electrical Safety Measures

Working with electrical systems requires special attention to avoid electrocution and other electrical hazards:

Power Off: Always disconnect power sources before working on electrical components. Use lockout/tag-out procedures to ensure the system remains off.

Insulation: Ensure all electrical wires and components are properly insulated and protected.

Testing: Use appropriate testing devices to verify that circuits are de-energized before touching them.

Dry Hands: Avoid working with electrical components while your hands or tools are wet.

Safe Handling of Refrigerants

Refrigerants are essential for HVAC systems but require careful handling due to their chemical properties and pressure:

Proper Storage: Store refrigerants in well-ventilated areas away from heat sources and direct sunlight.

Handling: Use appropriate personal protective equipment (PPE) such as gloves and goggles when handling refrigerants.

Disposal: Follow local regulations for the disposal and recycling of refrigerants to prevent environmental contamination.

Leak Detection: Regularly check for leaks and ensure any detected leaks are promptly addressed.

First Aid for HVAC Technicians

In case of an accident or injury, knowing basic first aid can be crucial:

Cuts and Abrasions: Clean the wound with water and apply an antiseptic. Cover with a sterile bandage.

Electrical Burns: If an electrical burn occurs, seek immediate medical attention. Avoid touching the affected area and ensure the power source is disconnected.

Heat Exhaustion: If someone shows signs of heat exhaustion, move them to a cooler environment, provide hydration, and seek medical attention if symptoms persist.

Safety Gear and PPE

Personal protective equipment (PPE) is essential for protecting HVAC technicians from potential hazards:

Gloves: Protect hands from sharp edges, hot surfaces, and chemicals.

Safety Glasses: Prevent eye injuries from debris, chemicals, or splashes.

Hard Hats: Wear when working in areas where falling objects or overhead hazards are present.

Respirators: Use when working with chemicals or in environments with poor air quality.

Emergency Procedures

Having a clear plan for emergencies can prevent confusion and ensure swift action:

Fire: Know the location of fire extinguishers and evacuation routes. In case of a fire, evacuate immediately and call emergency services.

Chemical Spills: Follow proper procedures for containing and cleaning up spills. Use the correct PPE and consult the Material Safety Data Sheet (MSDS) for guidance.

Injuries: Provide first aid as needed and seek medical attention for serious injuries. Report all incidents to the appropriate authorities and document them for future reference.

Chapter 5: Basic Principles

Principles of Thermodynamics

Thermodynamics is fundamental to understanding how HVAC systems work. It involves the study of heat and energy transfer, and it is governed by several key laws:

First Law of Thermodynamics (Law of Energy Conservation): Energy cannot be created or destroyed, only transformed from one form to another. In HVAC systems, this principle explains how energy is transferred between the refrigerant, air, and other system components.

Second Law of Thermodynamics: Heat naturally flows from a high-temperature area to a low-temperature area. This principle underpins the operation of heat pumps and air conditioners, which move heat against its natural flow direction.

Third Law of Thermodynamics: As the temperature of a system approaches absolute zero, the entropy (disorder) of the system approaches a constant minimum. This law is more theoretical but provides insight into low-temperature refrigeration processes.

Heat Transfer Mechanisms

Understanding how heat is transferred is crucial for designing and operating efficient HVAC systems. There are three primary mechanisms:

Conduction: The transfer of heat through a material without the movement of the material itself. For example, heat is conducted through metal ducts or pipes.

Convection: The transfer of heat by the movement of fluids (liquids or gases). In HVAC systems, convection occurs when warm air circulates in a room, transferring heat from a heater or air conditioner.

Radiation: The transfer of heat through electromagnetic waves. Radiant heating systems use this principle to warm spaces directly through infrared radiation.

Fluid Dynamics

Fluid dynamics is the study of fluids (liquids and gases) in motion. It plays a significant role in HVAC systems, affecting airflow, pressure, and energy consumption:

Continuity Equation: Ensures that the mass flow rate of air or refrigerant remains constant throughout the system, crucial for balanced airflow and system efficiency.

Bernoulli's Principle: Describes how the speed of a fluid affects its pressure. In HVAC systems, this principle helps explain how airflow speeds up or slows down as it moves through ductwork.

Pressure Loss: Understanding pressure drops in ducts and filters is essential for designing systems that maintain adequate airflow and efficiency.

Psychrometrics Basics

Psychrometrics involves the study of air and its properties, including temperature, humidity, and pressure. Key concepts include:

Dry Bulb Temperature: The air temperature measured by a standard thermometer.

Wet Bulb Temperature: The temperature measured by a thermometer with a moistened bulb, indicates the cooling effect of evaporation.

Relative Humidity: The ratio of the current absolute humidity to the maximum possible at the given temperature, expressed as a percentage. It affects comfort and system performance.

Dew Point: The temperature at which air becomes saturated and water vapor begins to condense. It is crucial for controlling humidity levels in HVAC systems.

Energy Balance Concepts

Energy balance refers to the equilibrium between the energy entering and leaving a system. In HVAC systems, maintaining energy balance is essential for:

Heating/Cooling Loads: Calculating the amount of energy needed to maintain desired temperatures in a space.

Efficiency Analysis: Evaluating how efficiently energy is used and identifying areas for improvement.

System Sizing: Ensuring that HVAC equipment is appropriately sized to meet the energy demands of the space without excessive energy use.

Airflow and Ventilation Principles

Effective airflow and ventilation are crucial for maintaining indoor air quality and comfort:

Air Changes per Hour (ACH): The number of times the air in a room is replaced with fresh air each hour. This metric helps determine ventilation needs.

Velocity and Pressure: Managing the speed and pressure of air through ducts and vents ensures even distribution and comfort.

Ventilation Strategies: Includes natural ventilation (using windows and vents) and mechanical ventilation (using fans and air handling units) to bring fresh air into buildings and remove stale air.

Indoor Air Quality Basics

Maintaining good indoor air quality (IAQ) is vital for health and comfort:

Pollutants: Common indoor air pollutants include dust, mold, and volatile organic compounds (VOCs). HVAC systems can help control these through filtration and ventilation.

Ventilation: Proper ventilation helps reduce pollutant concentrations and maintain a healthy indoor environment.

Humidity Control: Managing humidity levels prevents mold growth and maintains comfort. HVAC systems often include humidifiers or dehumidifiers to regulate indoor humidity.

Book 2

Detailed HVAC Components

Chapter 6: Heating Solutions

Overview of Furnaces

Furnaces are a key component in many HVAC systems, providing essential heating to homes and buildings. Here's a detailed look at how they work and their types:

Definition and Function: Furnaces are designed to heat air that is then distributed throughout a building via ducts. They operate on various fuel types, including natural gas, propane, oil, or electricity.

Types of Furnaces:

Gas Furnaces: Use natural gas or propane as fuel. They are popular for their efficiency and cost-effectiveness.

Oil Furnaces: Use heating oil, which can be more suitable for areas without natural gas lines.

Electric Furnaces: Use electrical resistance to generate heat. They are often used in areas where other fuel sources are not available or feasible.

Key Components:

Heat Exchanger: Transfers heat from the combustion process to the air.

Blower: Moves the heated air through the duct system.

Thermostat: Controls the furnace by maintaining the desired temperature.

Boilers Explained

Boilers provide hot water or steam for heating purposes. They are especially effective in hydronic heating systems. Here's a closer look:

Definition and Function: Boilers heat water or generate steam to distribute heat throughout a building via radiators or baseboards. They can use various fuels, including natural gas, oil, or electricity.

Types of Boilers:

Combi Boilers: Provide both heating and hot water from a single unit.

System Boilers: Require a separate hot water storage tank but can offer a higher flow rate of hot water.

Regular Boilers: Also known as traditional boilers, these are suitable for homes with existing radiator systems.

Key Components:

Heat Exchanger: Similar to that in furnaces, it transfers heat from the combustion process to the water.

Expansion Tank: Manages the pressure changes in the system.

Circulator Pump: Moves the hot water through the system.

Heat Pump Systems

Heat pumps are versatile systems that can provide both heating and cooling. Here's an overview of how they work:

Definition and Function: Heat pumps transfer heat from one place to another using refrigerant and a compressor. They are highly efficient because they move heat rather than generate it.

Types of Heat Pumps:

Air Source Heat Pumps: Extract heat from the outside air and transfer it indoors. They are commonly used for moderate climates.

Ground Source (Geothermal) Heat Pumps: Extract heat from the ground using buried pipes. They are more efficient in extreme climates but have a higher installation cost.

Key Components:

Evaporator Coil: Absorbs heat from the air or ground.

Condenser Coil: Releases heat to the indoor air.

Reversing Valve: Allows the heat pump to switch between heating and cooling modes.

Radiant Heating Methods

Radiant heating systems provide warmth directly through surfaces like floors or walls. Here's how they work:

Definition and Function: Radiant heating systems deliver heat directly to objects and people in a room, rather than warming the air. This method can be more comfortable and energy-efficient.

Types of Radiant Heating:

Radiant Floor Heating: Uses electric cables or heated water tubes beneath the floor surface.

Radiant Panels: Installed in walls or ceilings to radiate heat into the room.

Key Components:

Heat Source: This can be electric, water-based, or another type of heating element.

Distribution System: In the case of floor heating, this includes pipes or cables embedded in the flooring.

Electric Heating Options

Electric heating provides a straightforward solution for many heating needs. Here's a breakdown of the available options:

Definition and Function: Electric heating systems convert electrical energy directly into heat. They are often used in areas where other fuel sources are unavailable.

Types of Electric Heating:

Baseboard Heaters: Installed along the baseboards of a room, they provide consistent, localized heating.

Electric Radiators: Mimic is the function of traditional radiators but uses electricity as the heating medium.

Electric Space Heaters: Portable units that can be used to heat individual rooms or areas.

Key Components:

Heating Elements: Electrical components that convert electrical energy into heat.

Thermostat: Controls the temperature settings for electric heating units.

Fuel Types and Efficiency

The choice of fuel type can greatly affect the efficiency and cost of heating systems:

Natural Gas: Popular for its efficiency and lower cost compared to oil or electricity. However, it requires a gas supply and proper venting.

Oil: Offers high heat output but can be more expensive and requires storage tanks.

Electricity: Provides convenience and ease of installation but can be costly to operate in areas with high electricity rates.

Efficiency Ratings: Look for systems with high Annual Fuel Utilization Efficiency (AFUE) ratings for furnaces and Boilers, and high Heating Seasonal Performance Factor (HSPF) ratings for heat pumps.

Installation and Maintenance

Proper installation and regular maintenance are crucial for ensuring the efficient and safe operation of heating systems:

Installation:

Professional Installation: Hire certified professionals to ensure proper setup and compliance with local codes.

System Sizing: Ensure that the heating system is appropriately sized for the space to maximize efficiency.

Maintenance:

Regular Checks: Perform annual inspections and tune-ups to maintain system efficiency and prevent breakdowns.

Filter Replacement: Regularly replace or clean filters to ensure optimal air quality and system performance.

System Cleaning: Clean components such as burners, coils, and vents to prevent buildup and ensure efficient operation.

Chapter 7: Ventilation Systems

Air Duct Configurations

Air ducts are essential for distributing heated or cooled air throughout a building. Their design and configuration greatly impact system efficiency and indoor air quality:

Duct Types:

Flexible Ducts: Made from a flexible material that can be easily routed through tight spaces. They are often used in residential systems but may be less durable.

Rigid Ducts: Made from metal or rigid plastic, these ducts offer greater durability and are typically used in commercial systems.

Duct Layouts:

Branch Duct Systems: Common in residential setups, where a main duct branches out to various rooms.

Trunk and Branch Systems: More complex systems with a central trunk duct that branches into smaller ducts leading to different rooms.

Plenum Systems: Use large, central ducts (plenums) to distribute air to smaller ducts, often found in commercial buildings.

Design Considerations:

Airflow Efficiency: Ensure that ducts are properly sized and insulated to minimize energy loss and improve efficiency.

Minimizing Noise: Use soundproofing materials and design techniques to reduce duct noise.

Ventilation Fans

Ventilation fans are critical for maintaining air quality and comfort by removing stale air and introducing fresh air:

Types of Ventilation Fans:

Exhaust Fans: Commonly used in bathrooms and kitchens to remove moisture, odors, and pollutants.

Inline Fans: Installed within the ductwork, these fans provide powerful ventilation without being visible.

WholeHouse Fans: Used to ventilate an entire home by pulling cool outdoor air in through windows and exhausting warm indoor air through attic vents.

Key Features:

Fan Speed Control: Adjustable speeds allow for customized ventilation based on the needs of the space.

Noise Levels: Consider fans with low noise ratings for a quieter operation.

Installation Tips:

Proper Placement: Install fans in areas where moisture and pollutants are likely to accumulate.

Ventilation Ducting: Ensure that ducting is properly sealed and insulated to prevent energy loss.

Air Exchangers and HRV/ERV Systems

Heat Recovery Ventilators (HRVs) and Energy Recovery Ventilators (ERVs) enhance ventilation efficiency by transferring heat and moisture between incoming and outgoing air:

Heat Recovery Ventilators (HRVs):

Function: Transfer heat from outgoing stale air to incoming fresh air, reducing heating costs.

Operation: Ideal for colder climates where maintaining indoor heat is crucial.

Energy Recovery Ventilators (ERVs):

Function: Transfer both heat and moisture between incoming and outgoing air, which helps in maintaining balanced humidity levels.

Operation: Useful in both cold and hot climates, as they help regulate humidity in addition to temperature.

Key Components:

Heat Exchange Core: Where the heat or energy transfer takes place.

Fans: Used to move air through the system.

Filters: Help to remove dust and contaminants from the incoming air.

Natural vs. Mechanical Ventilation

Ventilation systems can be broadly classified into natural and mechanical methods, each with its advantages and applications:

Natural Ventilation:

Definition: Relies on natural forces like wind and temperature differences to circulate air.

Techniques: Includes opening windows, and vents, and using architectural features like skylights to enhance airflow.

Advantages: Cost-effective and energy-efficient. It leverages natural air movement without the need for mechanical systems.

Mechanical Ventilation:

Definition: Uses powered systems like fans and air handlers to control airflow.

Types:

Exhaust Ventilation: Removes indoor air using fans and relies on natural air infiltration for fresh air.

Supply Ventilation: Uses fans to introduce fresh air into a building, creating a positive pressure that pushes out stale air.

Balanced Ventilation: Employs both supply and exhaust fans to maintain neutral pressure and ensure proper air exchange.

Indoor Air Quality Enhancements

Improving indoor air quality (IAQ) is essential for comfort and health. Ventilation systems play a crucial role in this:

Air Purification: Integrate air filters and purifiers to remove airborne contaminants such as dust, pollen, and mold spores.

Humidity Control: Use dehumidifiers or humidifiers to maintain optimal humidity levels and prevent issues like mold growth and dry skin.

Ventilation Rates: Ensure adequate ventilation rates to reduce concentrations of indoor pollutants and improve overall air quality.

Ventilation for Different Environments

Different environments have specific ventilation needs based on their use and occupancy:

Residential Spaces:

General Ventilation: Focus on maintaining good air quality and comfort through balanced ventilation systems.

Special Areas: Bathrooms, kitchens, and laundry rooms require additional ventilation to handle moisture and odors.

Commercial Buildings:

Enhanced Ventilation: Larger buildings may require more sophisticated systems with higher capacity to handle the increased load of occupants and equipment.

Local Exhaust: Specific areas like laboratories or workshops may need localized exhaust systems to remove contaminants at the source.

Industrial Settings:

HighVolume Ventilation: Industrial environments often need high-volume ventilation systems to handle large amounts of air and remove pollutants effectively.

Safety Considerations: Ensure that ventilation systems meet industry safety standards and regulations to protect workers.

Maintenance and Troubleshooting

Regular maintenance and troubleshooting are essential to ensure that ventilation systems operate efficiently and effectively:

Routine Maintenance:

Duct Cleaning: Periodically clean ducts to remove dust and debris that can hinder airflow.

Fan Inspection: Check and lubricate fan blades and motors to ensure smooth operation.

Troubleshooting Common Issues:

Inadequate Ventilation: Check for blockages in ducts or filters and ensure that fans and vents are functioning properly.

Excessive Noise: Investigate potential causes such as loose parts, obstructions, or worn bearings.

Airflow Problems: Ensure that ductwork is properly sealed and insulated and that vents are unobstructed.

Chapter 8: Cooling Systems

Types of Air Conditioners

Air conditioners are essential for maintaining comfort in both residential and commercial settings. They come in various types, each suited to different needs and applications:

Window Air Conditioners:

Definition: Compact units installed in a window opening, ideal for cooling single rooms.

Features: Include built-in fans and thermostats. They are relatively easy to install and remove.

Advantages: Cost-effective for small spaces, easy to install.

Disadvantages: Can be noisy and block natural light from windows.

Split Air Conditioners:

Definition: Consists of two separate units – an indoor evaporator and an outdoor condenser.

Features: Allow for cooling multiple rooms with a single outdoor unit.

Advantages: Quiet operation and more efficient than window units.

Disadvantages: Requires professional installation and can be more expensive.

Packaged Air Conditioners:

Definition: All components are housed in a single unit, typically installed on the roof or a ground-level platform.

Features: Include both cooling and heating options (in some models).

Advantages: Saves space inside the building and is ideal for commercial applications.

Disadvantages: Requires a significant amount of space outside the building and can be less efficient for smaller spaces.

Central Air Conditioners:

Definition: Use a network of ducts to distribute cool air throughout a building.

Features: Typically include a large outdoor unit and an indoor air handler.

Advantages: Efficiently cools large areas and maintains a consistent temperature.

Disadvantages: Higher installation costs and requires ductwork.

Evaporative Cooling Systems

Evaporative cooling systems use the natural process of water evaporation to cool air, offering an energy-efficient alternative to traditional air conditioning:

Definition and Function: Evaporative coolers (also known as swamp coolers) draw warm air through water-saturated pads, cooling it by evaporation before distributing it through the space.

Types of Evaporative Coolers:

Direct Evaporative Coolers: Pass air directly over wet pads, adding moisture to the air and cooling it.

Indirect Evaporative Coolers: Use a heat exchanger to cool the air without adding moisture, suitable for more humid climates.

Key Components:

Water Pump: Circulates water to the cooling pads.

Cooling Pads: Water-saturated pads where evaporation occurs.

Fan: Moves the cooled air into the living space.

Advantages:

Energy Efficiency: Uses less energy than traditional air conditioning systems.

CostEffective: Lower initial costs and operational expenses.

Disadvantages:

Humidity Addition: This can increase indoor humidity, which may not be suitable for very humid climates.

Maintenance: Requires regular cleaning and water treatment to prevent mold and scale buildup.

Split and Packaged Units

Split and packaged units are two primary configurations for air conditioning systems, each with specific applications and benefits:

Split Units:

Definition: Consists of an indoor evaporator unit and an outdoor condenser unit connected by refrigerant lines.

Applications: Ideal for residential and small commercial spaces where ductwork is not feasible.

Advantages: Quiet operation, flexibility in zoning, and efficient cooling for individual rooms or areas.

Packaged Units:

Definition: All components are contained in a single unit, typically installed outside the building.

Applications: Commonly used in commercial buildings and large homes where space inside is limited.

Advantages: Simplified installation, saves indoor space, and can include both cooling and heating functions.

Chiller Systems

Chiller systems are used in large cooling applications, such as commercial buildings and industrial processes:

Definition and Function: Chillers use refrigeration cycles to remove heat from a liquid (typically water or glycol) and then circulate this chilled liquid through the building for cooling.

Types of Chillers:

AirCooled Chillers: Use air to dissipate heat from the refrigerant.

WaterCooled Chillers: Use water from a cooling tower to remove heat, which is more efficient but requires additional infrastructure.

Key Components:

Compressor: Compresses the refrigerant and circulates it through the system.

Evaporator: Removes heat from the liquid being cooled.

Condenser: Releases heat to the surrounding environment.

Advantages:

Efficiency: Suitable for large cooling needs with high efficiency.
Flexibility: Can be used in a variety of applications, including HVAC systems, industrial processes, and more.

Cooling Towers

Cooling towers are used to reject heat from a chiller system or other industrial processes into the atmosphere:

Definition and Function: Cooling towers use the principle of evaporation to cool water, which is then recirculated in the system.

Types of Cooling Towers:

Counterflow Cooling Towers: Air flows vertically upward through the falling water.
Crossflow Cooling Towers: Air flows horizontally through the falling water.

Key Components:

Fill Material: Increases the surface area for heat exchange.
Fans: Move air through the tower to aid in the cooling process.
Drift Eliminators: Reduce the loss of water droplets with the exhaust air.

Advantages:

High Efficiency: Effective for large cooling applications.
CostEffective: Lower operating costs compared to other cooling methods.

Refrigeration Cycles

Refrigeration cycles are the fundamental process behind many cooling systems, including air conditioners and refrigerators:

Definition and Function: The refrigeration cycle involves the transfer of heat from a low-temperature area to a high-temperature area, using a refrigerant that undergoes phase changes.

Types of Refrigeration Cycles:

Vapor Compression Cycle: The most common cycle, where a refrigerant is compressed, condensed, expanded, and evaporated.
Absorption Cycle: Uses heat to drive the refrigeration process, often used in large-scale or industrial applications.

Key Components:

Compressor: Compresses the refrigerant gas.
Condenser: Cools and condenses the refrigerant.
Expansion Valve: Reduces the pressure of the refrigerant.
Evaporator: Absorbs heat from the surroundings.

Seasonal Energy Efficiency

Seasonal energy efficiency is a crucial factor in determining the overall performance and cost-effectiveness of cooling systems:

Seasonal Energy Efficiency Ratio (SEER):

Definition: Measures the cooling efficiency of an air conditioner over an entire cooling season.
Calculation: SEER is calculated by dividing the total cooling output (in BTUs) by the total energy input (in watt-hours).

Coefficient of Performance (COP):

Definition: Measures the efficiency of heating and cooling systems by comparing the amount of heating or cooling provided to the amount of energy consumed.
Application: Higher COP values indicate greater efficiency.

Energy Star Ratings:

Definition: Indicates products that meet specific energy efficiency criteria set by the Environmental Protection Agency (EPA).
Benefits: Energy Star-rated systems often provide cost savings and environmental benefits.

Chapter 9: Controls and Thermostats

Thermostat Types

Thermostats are crucial for regulating HVAC systems and maintaining comfortable indoor temperatures. They come in various types, each offering unique features and benefits:

Mechanical Thermostats:

Definition: Use physical components like bimetallic strips or mercury switches to control temperature.

Features: Simple and reliable, often found in older systems.

Advantages: Cost-effective and straightforward to use.

Disadvantages: Limited functionality and less precise temperature control.

Digital Thermostats:

Definition: Use electronic sensors and digital displays to control temperature settings.

Features: Offer more precise temperature control and can be programmed for different schedules.

Advantages: Greater accuracy and ease of use.

Disadvantages: May require battery changes or electrical power.

Programmable Thermostats:

Definition: Allow users to set temperature schedules for different times of the day and week.

Features: This can be programmed to adjust temperatures based on occupancy and time.

Advantages: Can reduce energy consumption by optimizing heating and cooling schedules.

Disadvantages: May be complex to program for some users.

Smart Thermostats:

Definition: Connect to the internet and can be controlled remotely via smartphones or voice assistants.

Features: Learn user preferences and adjust settings automatically. They can also integrate with other smart home devices.

Advantages: Enhanced control and energy savings through adaptive learning and remote access.

Disadvantages: Higher initial cost and dependency on internet connectivity.

Smart Control Systems

Smart control systems enhance the functionality and efficiency of HVAC systems through advanced technology:

Definition and Function: Utilize internet connectivity and sophisticated algorithms to optimize HVAC operations, improve energy efficiency, and provide user-friendly controls.

Key Features:

Remote Access: Control HVAC systems from anywhere using smartphones or computers.

Adaptive Learning: Systems learn user habits and adjust settings accordingly to maximize comfort and efficiency.

Integration with Other Systems: Smart controls can integrate with home automation systems, including lighting, security, and energy management.

Advantages:
Convenience: Allows for remote monitoring and control.
Efficiency: This can help reduce energy consumption through intelligent scheduling and optimization.
Disadvantages:
Complexity: This may require an initial setup and a learning curve.
Cost: Higher initial investment compared to traditional controls.

Zoning and Building Automation Systems

Zoning and building automation systems provide advanced control over HVAC operations in large or multiuse buildings:
Zoning Systems:
Definition: Divide a building into different zones, each with its temperature control.
Features: Use multiple thermostats and dampers to manage temperatures in different areas.
Advantages: Improved comfort and energy efficiency by tailoring climate control to individual needs.
Building Automation Systems (BAS):
Definition: Centralized systems that manage various building functions, including HVAC, lighting, and security.
Features: Integrate different systems into a single interface for easier management.
Advantages: Enhanced operational efficiency and centralized control.
Integration:
Coordination: BAS can coordinate HVAC operations with other building systems for optimized performance.
Monitoring: Provide real-time data and alerts for system performance and maintenance needs.

Sensors and Actuators

Sensors and actuators play crucial roles in the operation of HVAC systems by providing feedback and controlling various components:
Sensors:
Temperature Sensors: Measure the current temperature and provide data to the thermostat or control system.
Humidity Sensors: Monitor indoor humidity levels and adjust system operation to maintain comfort.
Air Quality Sensors: Detect pollutants or contaminants and trigger ventilation or filtration systems as needed.
Actuators:
Definition: Devices that perform physical actions based on control signals, such as opening or closing dampers.
Types:
Electric Actuators: Use electrical power to operate mechanical components.
Pneumatic Actuators: Use compressed air for actuation.

Integration:
Coordination: Sensors provide data to controllers, which use actuators to adjust system components accordingly.
Feedback: Ensures accurate and responsive control based on real-time conditions.

Control Strategies

Effective control strategies are essential for optimizing HVAC performance and ensuring energy efficiency:

On/Off Control:
Definition: Basic control method where the system alternates between fully on and off states.
Advantages: Simple and reliable.
Disadvantages: This can lead to temperature swings and reduced efficiency.

Modulating Control:
Definition: Adjusts the system's output gradually based on current conditions.
Advantages: Provides more precise temperature control and improved efficiency.
Disadvantages: More complex and may require advanced equipment.

Adaptive Control:
Definition: Uses algorithms to learn and adapt to user preferences and environmental conditions.
Advantages: Optimizes performance and energy usage over time.
Disadvantages: Requires sophisticated control systems and initial setup.

Energy Management Systems

Energy management systems (EMS) help monitor and control energy usage to reduce costs and improve efficiency:

Definition and Function: Systems that track energy consumption, analyze data, and provide recommendations for improving energy efficiency.

Key Features:
RealTime Monitoring: Track energy use and system performance in real time.
Data Analysis: Analyze consumption patterns and identify areas for improvement.
Optimization: Provide recommendations for energy-saving measures and adjustments.

Advantages:
Cost Savings: Reduce energy costs through efficient management and optimization.
Environmental Impact: Lower energy consumption reduces carbon footprint.

Disadvantages:
Initial Cost: This may require investment in technology and setup.
Complexity: Implementing and managing an EMS can be complex.

Integration with Smart Home Devices

Integrating HVAC controls with smart home devices enhances convenience and efficiency:

Definition and Function: Connect HVAC systems with smart home devices such as voice assistants, smart lighting, and security systems.

Key Benefits:

Convenience: Control HVAC systems using voice commands or smartphone apps.

Efficiency: Synchronize HVAC operation with other smart devices to optimize energy use.

Automation: Set up routines or schedules that coordinate HVAC with other home functions.

Challenges:

Compatibility: Ensure that all devices are compatible and can communicate effectively.

Security: Protect connected systems from potential cybersecurity threats.

Book 3

Techniques for HVAC installation

Chapter 10: Pre-Installation Planning

Design and Planning Considerations

Before beginning an HVAC installation, meticulous planning is essential to ensure the system functions efficiently and meets the needs of the space:

Understanding Requirements: Determine the specific heating, cooling, and ventilation needs based on the type of building (residential or commercial), occupancy, and usage patterns.

System Selection: Choose the appropriate HVAC system type (e.g., split, packaged, ductless) based on the design requirements and building layout.

Layout Design: Plan the placement of HVAC components, including indoor and outdoor units, ductwork, and vents, to optimize performance and minimize disruptions to the building's structure.

Load Calculation and Sizing

Accurate load calculations are crucial for selecting the right HVAC system size:

Heat Load Calculation: Assess the amount of heat energy required to maintain desired indoor temperatures. Factors include insulation levels, window sizes, and outdoor climate.

Cooling Load Calculation: Determine the cooling capacity needed to counteract heat gain from sunlight, appliances, and occupants.

Manual J Calculation: Use industry-standard software or guidelines to perform detailed load calculations. This ensures the system size matches the building's needs.

Environmental Impact Assessments

Evaluating the environmental impact of the HVAC system helps in choosing eco-friendly options and ensuring compliance with regulations:

Energy Efficiency: Consider systems with high Seasonal Energy Efficiency Ratio (SEER) and Annual Fuel Utilization Efficiency (AFUE) ratings to reduce energy consumption.

Refrigerants: Choose HVAC systems that use low-impact refrigerants with minimal ozone-depleting potential.

Sustainable Practices: Implement practices such as proper insulation and duct sealing to improve overall energy efficiency and reduce environmental impact.

Budgeting and Cost Estimation

Developing a detailed budget helps manage costs and ensures financial feasibility for the HVAC installation:

Cost Breakdown: Include expenses for equipment, labor, materials, permits, and any additional features or upgrades.

Estimates: Obtain multiple quotes from contractors to compare costs and ensure competitive pricing.

Contingency Funds: Allocate a portion of the budget for unexpected expenses or modifications during installation.

Permits and Regulations

Compliance with local codes and regulations is essential for a successful installation:

Building Codes: Review and adhere to local building codes and HVAC installation standards.

Permits: Obtain necessary permits from local authorities before beginning the installation process.

Inspection Requirements: Schedule inspections as required by local regulations to ensure the installation meets all safety and performance standards.

Site Preparation

Proper site preparation is crucial for a smooth and efficient HVAC installation:

Access: Ensure there is adequate access for installing equipment, especially for large or heavy components.

Clearing Space: Remove any obstructions that could interfere with the installation process or the operation of the HVAC system.

Infrastructure: Verify that electrical and plumbing systems are in place and meet the requirements for the new HVAC system.

Scheduling and Logistics

Effective scheduling and logistics planning help ensure the installation proceeds smoothly and on time:

Timeline: Develop a detailed installation timeline that includes all phases of the project, from equipment delivery to final testing.

Coordination: Coordinate with contractors, suppliers, and other stakeholders to ensure all parties are aligned with the project schedule.

Contingency Planning: Prepare for potential delays or issues by having contingency plans in place to address unforeseen challenges.

Chapter 11: Heating System Installation

Steps for Furnace Installation

Installing a furnace involves several critical steps to ensure it operates efficiently and safely. Here's a comprehensive guide:

Preparation:

Site Assessment: Evaluate the installation site to ensure it meets clearance, ventilation, and accessibility requirements.

Equipment Arrival: Verify the furnace and components are delivered intact and ready for installation.

Removing the Old Furnace (if applicable):

Turn Off Utilities: Shut off electrical and gas supplies to the old unit.

Dismantle: Carefully remove the old furnace, including disconnecting and removing associated ductwork and components.

Installing the New Furnace:

Placement: Position the new furnace in the designated area, ensuring it is level and properly aligned.

Mounting: Secure the furnace as per manufacturer instructions, using appropriate supports and anchors.

Connecting Ductwork and Ventilation:

Duct Connections: Attach the furnace to existing or new ductwork, ensuring all connections are sealed and properly aligned.

Ventilation: Install the venting system to safely expel combustion gases outside. Ensure proper clearance and secure all fittings.

Electrical and Gas Connections:

Electrical Wiring: Connect the furnace to the electrical system, following the manufacturer's wiring diagram. Ensure all connections are insulated and secure.

Gas Line: Connect the gas line to the furnace, checking for leaks with a gas leak detector and ensuring all connections are tight.

Thermostat Installation:

Location: Install the thermostat in a central location, away from heat sources or drafts.

Wiring: Connect the thermostat to the furnace, ensuring proper wiring according to the manufacturer's guidelines.

Testing and Calibration:

System Operation: Test the furnace to ensure it starts, runs, and shuts off correctly. Check for proper airflow and heating efficiency.

Safety Checks: Verify that all safety features, such as limit switches and flame sensors, are functioning properly.

Boiler Installation Guidelines

Installing a boiler requires careful attention to detail for efficiency and safety:

Site Preparation:

Space Requirements: Ensure the boiler is installed on a stable, level surface with sufficient clearance for maintenance.

Flooring: Verify the flooring can support the boiler's weight and that it is suitable for water or fuel spills.

Mounting and Positioning:

Placement: Position the boiler according to the manufacturer's specifications, considering access for maintenance and servicing.

Securing: Anchor the boiler securely to prevent movement and ensure stability.

Piping Connections:

Water Supply and Return: Connect the boiler to the water supply and return lines, ensuring all connections are properly sealed and aligned.

Ventilation: Install the boiler's venting system to safely expel combustion gases. Ensure all connections are secure and leak-free.

Electrical Connections:

Wiring: Connect the boiler to the electrical system, following the manufacturer's wiring diagram and ensuring all connections are insulated.

Controls: Install any control systems or thermostats as required.

Filling and Purging:

Water Filling: Fill the boiler with water, checking for leaks in the piping system.

Air Purging: Purge air from the system to ensure proper operation and prevent airlocks.

Testing and Commissioning:

Operational Test: Run the boiler through a complete heating cycle to ensure it operates correctly and efficiently.

Safety Checks: Verify that all safety controls, such as pressure relief valves and temperature sensors, are functioning correctly.

Radiant Floor Heating Setup

Radiant floor heating systems offer comfort and efficiency. The setup involves several key steps:

Planning and Design:

Layout: Design the layout of the heating elements (e.g., tubing or electric mats) based on the room dimensions and heating needs.

Insulation: Install insulation beneath the heating elements to improve efficiency and minimize heat loss.

Installation:

Subfloor Preparation: Prepare the subfloor by cleaning and leveling it to ensure proper installation of heating elements.

Heating Element Placement: Install the heating elements according to the design layout, ensuring correct spacing and alignment.

Connection and Wiring:

Water or Electric Connection: Connect the heating elements to the water supply or electrical system, ensuring all connections are secure and compliant with codes.

Thermostat Installation: Install the thermostat to control the radiant floor heating system.

Testing and Commissioning:

System Check: Test the system to ensure even heating and proper operation.

Adjustments: Make necessary adjustments to the thermostat or heating elements for optimal performance.

Heat Pump Installation Process

Heat pumps provide versatile heating and cooling solutions. The installation process includes:

Site Selection:

Outdoor Unit Placement: Choose a location with adequate clearance and ventilation for the outdoor unit.

Indoor Unit Placement: Position the indoor unit to ensure efficient air distribution and accessibility.

Mounting and Securing:

Outdoor Unit: Mount the outdoor unit on a stable surface, such as a concrete pad or wall bracket.

Indoor Unit: Install the indoor unit according to manufacturer guidelines.

Refrigerant Lines and Electrical Connections:

Line Connections: Connect the refrigerant lines between the indoor and outdoor units, ensuring proper sealing and insulation.

Electrical Wiring: Connect the heat pump to the electrical system, following the manufacturer's wiring diagram.

Thermostat and Controls:

Installation: Install the thermostat and any control systems, ensuring proper connections and functionality.

Programming: Set up the thermostat for heating and cooling schedules.

Testing and Calibration:

System Operation: Test the heat pump to ensure it operates correctly in both heating and cooling modes.

Efficiency Check: Adjust settings for optimal performance and energy efficiency.

Fuel Supply Connections

Properly connecting the fuel supply is essential for safe and efficient heating system operation:

Gas Lines:

Connection: Connect gas lines to the heating system, ensuring all fittings are secure and leak-free.

Leak Testing: Use a gas leak detector to check for leaks and ensure safe operation.

Oil Lines:
Connection: Connect oil lines to the heating system, ensuring proper alignment and sealing.
Filter Installation: Install oil filters to prevent contaminants from entering the system.
Electrical Supply:
Wiring: Ensure all electrical connections are properly insulated and secure.
Power Supply: Verify the system is connected to a reliable power source.

Testing and Commissioning

Thorough testing and commissioning ensure the heating system operates effectively and safely:
System Check:
Operational Test: Run the system through a full heating cycle to ensure proper operation.
Performance Evaluation: Measure performance metrics such as temperature and airflow to ensure efficiency.
Safety Checks:
Safety Features: Verify that all safety features, such as limit switches and safety valves, are functioning correctly.
Leak Detection: Inspect for any fuel, refrigerant, or air leaks.

Troubleshooting Installation Issues

Addressing common installation issues ensures the system operates correctly:
Common Problems:
Inadequate Heating/Cooling: Check for issues such as incorrect sizing, poor insulation, or improper ductwork.
Noise Issues: Investigate potential causes such as loose components, improper installation, or system imbalances.
Resolution
Adjustments: Make necessary adjustments to system settings or components.
Repairs: Perform repairs or replacements as needed to address issues.

Chapter 12: Air Conditioning Installation

Installing Indoor and Outdoor Units
Indoor Unit Installation:
Location Selection: Choose a location for the indoor unit that allows for optimal air distribution and accessibility for maintenance. Ensure it's away from direct sunlight, heat sources, and obstacles.
Mounting: Securely mount the indoor unit on a wall or ceiling using appropriate brackets and supports. Ensure it is level and correctly aligned.
Drainage: Install a condensate drain line to remove excess moisture from the unit. Ensure the drain line is properly sloped to prevent water pooling.
Outdoor Unit Installation:
Site Preparation: Place the outdoor unit on a stable surface, such as a concrete pad or a mounting bracket. Ensure it has adequate clearance for airflow and maintenance access.
Mounting: Secure the outdoor unit using appropriate supports and anchors. Ensure it is level and positioned to avoid obstructing airflow.
Connection: Connect the refrigerant lines, ensuring all fittings are tight and leak-free. Connect the power supply as per manufacturer instructions.

Ductwork Installation Procedures
Design and Planning:
Duct Layout: Design the duct system to ensure even airflow throughout the space. Plan for main ducts, branch ducts, and registers to provide balanced air distribution.
Sizing: Use appropriate duct sizing calculations to ensure optimal airflow and system efficiency.
Installation:
Duct Assembly: Assemble and install ductwork, ensuring all joints and connections are sealed with duct tape or mastic to prevent air leaks.
Support: Secure ducts with appropriate hangers and supports to prevent sagging and ensure proper alignment.
Insulation: Insulate ducts in unconditioned spaces to prevent energy loss and condensation. Ensure insulation is properly applied and secured.
Connecting Ductwork:
Registers and Grilles: Install registers and grilles at the appropriate locations, ensuring they are properly aligned and secured.
Sealing: Ensure all duct connections are sealed and tested for leaks.

Setting Up Mini Split Systems

Indoor Unit Installation:

Mounting: Install the indoor unit on a wall or ceiling, ensuring it is level and properly supported. Avoid locations with obstructions to airflow.

Connection: Connect the indoor unit to the outdoor unit using refrigerant lines and electrical wiring, following the manufacturer's instructions.

Outdoor Unit Installation:

Placement: Position the outdoor unit on a stable surface with adequate clearance for airflow and maintenance.

Connection: Connect refrigerant lines, electrical wiring, and drainage lines between the indoor and outdoor units.

Testing:

System Check: Test the system to ensure proper operation, including heating and cooling modes. Check for leaks in refrigerant lines and ensure all connections are secure.

Chiller Installation Steps

Site Preparation:

Location: Choose a location for the chiller that provides adequate space for installation, maintenance, and ventilation.

Foundation: Prepare a stable foundation or pad to support the chiller's weight and ensure proper leveling.

Mounting:

Positioning: Position the chiller on the foundation, ensuring it is level and properly aligned.

Securing: Anchor the chiller to the foundation using appropriate supports and fasteners.

Connecting Piping:

Water Lines: Connect the chiller to the water supply and return lines, ensuring all fittings are secure and leak-free.

Refrigerant Lines: Connect refrigerant lines to the chiller, following the manufacturer's guidelines.

Electrical Connections:

Wiring: Connect the chiller to the electrical supply, ensuring all wiring is properly insulated and secure. Follow the manufacturer's electrical schematics.

Testing and Commissioning:

System Operation: Run the chiller through a complete cooling cycle to ensure it operates correctly and efficiently.

Performance Check: Verify that all operational parameters are within the manufacturer's specifications and adjust settings as needed.

Refrigerant Charging

Preparation:

Tools and Equipment: Gather the necessary tools, including a refrigerant gauge set, vacuum pump, and refrigerant cylinders.

System Check: Ensure the system is properly evacuated and free of air and moisture before charging with refrigerant.

Charging Process:

Connect Gauges: Attach the refrigerant gauges to the service ports of the system.

Add Refrigerant: Slowly add refrigerant to the system, monitoring the pressure and temperature to ensure it matches the manufacturer's specifications.

Adjust: Make any necessary adjustments to the refrigerant charge based on system performance and gauge readings.

Final Checks:

Leak Test: Check for any leaks in the refrigerant lines and connections.

System Operation: Verify that the system is operating correctly and efficiently after charging.

Electrical Connections

Power Supply:

Connection: Connect the system to the electrical power supply, ensuring all connections are secure and compliant with electrical codes.

Circuit Protection: Install circuit breakers or fuses as required by the manufacturer's specifications.

Control Wiring:

Thermostat Wiring: Connect the thermostat to the HVAC system, following the manufacturer's wiring diagram.

Control Wiring: Ensure all control wiring is properly connected and insulated.

Testing:

Power On: Turn on the power to the system and check for proper operation.

Safety Checks: Verify that all safety features, such as emergency shutoff switches, are functioning correctly.

System StartUp and Testing

Initial StartUp:

Power Up: Turn on the HVAC system and check for proper startup and operation of all components.

Calibration: Adjust settings and calibrate the system as necessary to ensure optimal performance.

Performance Testing:

Cooling Performance: Test the system's cooling capacity and airflow to ensure it meets performance specifications.

Efficiency Check: Measure system efficiency and verify that it operates within the manufacturer's guidelines.

Final Inspection:

System Review: Inspect all components, connections, and settings to ensure everything is functioning correctly.

Documentation: Complete any necessary documentation and provide the customer with information on system operation and maintenance.

Chapter 13: Ventilation System Installation

Installing Exhaust Systems
Planning and Design:
Location Selection: Identify optimal locations for exhaust fans or systems to effectively remove contaminants from specific areas such as kitchens, bathrooms, or industrial spaces.
Capacity Requirements: Determine the required exhaust capacity based on the size of the space and the level of contaminants to be removed.
Installation:
Mounting: Install exhaust fans or systems securely, ensuring they are mounted correctly and aligned with ductwork. Use appropriate mounting hardware and brackets.
Ductwork Connection: Connect the exhaust system to the ductwork, ensuring all joints are sealed to prevent air leaks. Use insulated ducting if necessary to reduce noise and improve efficiency.
Ventilation Outlets: Ensure the exhaust outlets are properly vented to the outside, avoiding obstructions that could impede airflow.
Testing and Adjustment:
System Check: Test the exhaust system to ensure it operates correctly, providing adequate airflow and effectively removing contaminants.
Adjustments: Make necessary adjustments to fan speeds or duct configurations to optimize performance.

Fresh Air Intake Methods
Direct Intake:
Location: Install intake vents in areas where fresh air can be drawn in without being contaminated by pollutants or debris. Consider locations such as high up on walls or near clean outdoor environments.
Screening: Install filters or screens on intake vents to prevent the entry of debris and pests.
Mechanical Fresh Air Systems:
Installation: Install mechanical fresh air systems, such as air handlers or energy recovery ventilators (ERVs), to provide controlled fresh air intake. Ensure proper placement for efficient operation.
Connection: Connect the fresh air system to the existing HVAC system or ductwork as per manufacturer instructions.
Balanced Ventilation:
Integration: Integrate fresh air intake systems with existing ventilation to ensure a balanced approach that avoids negative pressure or drafts in the building.
Monitoring: Monitor airflow and air quality to ensure the system maintains a consistent and adequate supply of fresh air.

Whole House Ventilation Solutions

System Types:

Heat Recovery Ventilators (HRVs): Install HRVs to exchange stale indoor air with fresh outdoor air while recovering heat energy to maintain temperature.

Energy Recovery Ventilators (ERVs): Install ERVs for similar benefits as HRVs but also manage humidity levels in addition to heat recovery.

Ductwork Design:

Layout: Design ductwork to ensure even distribution of fresh air throughout the house. Use balanced duct configurations to avoid areas with poor air circulation.

Insulation: Insulate ductwork in unconditioned spaces to reduce energy loss and improve efficiency.

System Installation:

Mounting and Connection: Install the whole house ventilation system and connect it to the ductwork. Ensure all connections are secure and airtight.

Testing: Test the system to verify proper operation and balanced airflow throughout the house.

Ductless Ventilation Options

Types of Ductless Systems:

Ductless Range Hoods: Install ductless range hoods over cooking surfaces to capture and filter kitchen fumes before recirculating clean air back into the kitchen.

Portable Air Purifiers: Use portable air purifiers in individual rooms to improve indoor air quality without requiring ductwork.

Installation:

Mounting: Install ductless ventilation units according to manufacturer guidelines. Ensure proper positioning for effective air capture and filtration.

Filter Maintenance: Regularly clean or replace filters to maintain system efficiency and air quality.

Balancing Airflow

Airflow Measurement:

Tools and Techniques: Use tools such as anemometers or airflow meters to measure airflow rates in different areas of the ventilation system.

Adjustments: Adjust damper settings or fan speeds to balance airflow and ensure even distribution throughout the building.

System Balancing:

Ductwork Adjustments: Make necessary adjustments to ductwork to improve airflow balance, such as resizing ducts or adjusting bends and turns.

Ventilation Controls: Utilize ventilation controls or zoning systems to manage and balance airflow based on specific needs or occupancy levels.

Sound and Vibration Control

Soundproofing:

Materials: Use soundproofing materials such as acoustic panels or insulation to reduce noise from ventilation systems.

Installation: Install soundproofing materials around noisy components, such as fans or ductwork, to minimize noise transmission.

Vibration Control:

Vibration Isolation: Install vibration isolation pads or mounts to reduce vibrations transmitted from the ventilation system to the building structure.

Maintenance: Regularly check and maintain vibration control systems to ensure continued effectiveness.

Maintenance Access Considerations

Accessibility Planning:

Service Locations: Design and install ventilation systems with accessible service points for regular maintenance and repairs.

Clearances: Ensure adequate clearances around ventilation components to facilitate easy access for servicing.

Maintenance Procedures:

Routine Checks: Establish a maintenance schedule for regular inspection, cleaning, and servicing of ventilation systems.

Documentation: Maintain records of maintenance activities and any issues encountered to ensure the system operates efficiently and reliably.

Book 4

HVAC Maintenance and Problem-solving

Chapter 14: Routine Maintenance Tasks

Cleaning and Replacing Filters
Importance of Filters:
Air Quality: Filters are essential for maintaining indoor air quality by trapping dust, pollen, and other airborne particles.
System Efficiency: Clean filters ensure that HVAC systems operate efficiently by allowing unrestricted airflow.
Cleaning Procedures:
Type of Filter: Identify the type of filter in your system (e.g., HEPA, electrostatic, or fiberglass) and follow specific cleaning recommendations.
Removal and Cleaning: Turn off the system before removing the filter. Clean reusable filters with water or a vacuum, depending on the manufacturer's guidelines. Ensure filters are completely dry before reinstallation.
Replacing Filters: Frequency: Replace filters based on manufacturer recommendations, typically every 1 to 3 months, or more frequently if the system is used heavily or in dusty environments.
Selection: Choose the correct filter size and type for your HVAC system. Check the filter's MERV (Minimum Efficiency Reporting Value) rating to ensure it meets your air quality needs.

Conducting System Inspections
Inspection Checklist:
Visual Inspection: Examine all HVAC components for signs of wear, damage, or leakage. Check for visible issues such as frayed wires, rust, or loose connections.
Operational Check: Turn on the system and observe its operation. Listen for unusual noises and check for proper heating or cooling output.
Component Inspection:
Heating Elements: Inspect heating elements or burners for proper operation and cleanliness.
Cooling Coils: Check evaporator and condenser coils for dirt or debris that could impact performance.
Ductwork: Look for signs of leaks, disconnected ducts, or poor insulation.

Seasonal Maintenance Activities
Spring/Summer Maintenance:
Air Conditioning: Clean or replace filters, check refrigerant levels, inspect the condenser and evaporator coils, and ensure proper drainage of condensate lines.
Ductwork: Inspect and clean ductwork to remove dust and debris.
Fall/Winter Maintenance:
Heating Systems: Clean or replace filters, inspect the furnace or boiler, check for proper operation of heating elements, and ensure that vents and flues are clear.

Heat Exchangers: Check heat exchangers for signs of wear or damage, and ensure proper functioning.

Preventive Maintenance Strategies

Routine Checkups:

Scheduled Inspections: Establish a routine maintenance schedule, including regular inspections and servicing by a qualified technician.

System Calibration: Regularly calibrate thermostats and controls to ensure accurate temperature settings and efficient operation.

Component Maintenance:

Lubrication: Apply lubricant to moving parts such as fan motors and bearings to reduce friction and wear.

System Adjustments: Make necessary adjustments to system settings, such as airflow or temperature controls, to optimize performance.

Recordkeeping and Documentation

Maintenance Records:

Log Details: Maintain detailed records of all maintenance activities, including dates, tasks performed, and any issues encountered.

System History: Keep a history of repairs and replacements to track system performance and identify recurring issues.

Documentation:

Manuals and Warranties: Store manufacturer manuals and warranty information in an easily accessible location for reference.

Service Reports: Keep copies of service reports from professional technicians for future reference and warranty claims.

Scheduling and Planning

Maintenance Calendar:

Annual Schedule: Develop an annual maintenance calendar, outlining key tasks and deadlines for each season.

Reminders: Set up reminders for filter changes, inspections, and other routine maintenance tasks to ensure they are not overlooked.

Professional Services:

Technician Scheduling: Schedule periodic checkups and maintenance with a qualified HVAC technician to ensure comprehensive service and address any potential issues.

Emergency Planning: Have a plan in place for emergency repairs or service needs to minimize downtime and system disruptions.

Chapter 15: Identifying Common HVAC Problems

Troubles with Heating Systems
No Heat Production:
Possible Causes: Thermostat issues, tripped circuit breakers, or a faulty ignition system.
Diagnosis: Check thermostat settings, reset circuit breakers, and inspect the ignition system or pilot light. Ensure the system is set to "heat" mode.
Inconsistent Heating:
Possible Causes: Clogged filters, ductwork leaks, or uneven airflow.
Strange Noises:
Possible Causes: Loose or damaged components, worn-out bearings, or airflow obstructions.
Diagnosis: Listen for specific noises (e.g., banging, squealing) and inspect components for wear or damage. Tighten loose parts and remove obstructions.
Short Cycling:
Possible Causes: Thermostat malfunctions, oversized equipment, or dirty filters.
Diagnosis: Verify thermostat accuracy, check system size compatibility, and replace filters if clogged.

Cooling System Issues
No Cool Air:
Possible Causes: Electrical issues, refrigerant problems, or compressor failures.
Diagnosis: Check electrical connections, ensure the refrigerant levels are adequate, and inspect the compressor for operational issues.
Reduced Cooling Efficiency:
Possible Causes: Dirty condenser coils, blocked air filters, or inadequate refrigerant levels.
Diagnosis: Clean condenser coils, replace air filters, and check refrigerant levels.
Ice Formation on Coils:
Possible Causes: Restricted airflow, low refrigerant, or faulty components.
Diagnosis: Check airflow around the evaporator coils, inspect refrigerant levels, and test for faulty components.
Strange Odors:
Possible Causes: Mold growth, burnt-out components, or foreign objects in the system.
Diagnosis: Inspect and clean the system to remove mold or debris, and check for burnt components.

Ventilation Challenges
Inadequate Ventilation:
Possible Causes: Blocked vents, undersized or poorly designed ductwork.
Diagnosis: Ensure vents are clear and unobstructed, and evaluate ductwork for proper sizing and design.

Uneven Air Distribution:
Possible Causes: Imbalanced ductwork, closed or obstructed vents.
Diagnosis: Check and adjust ductwork for balance, and ensure all vents are open and unobstructed.
Excess Humidity:
Possible Causes: Faulty ventilation fans, and inadequate air exchange.
Diagnosis: Test ventilation fans for proper operation, and check if the air exchange rate is sufficient.

Electrical Faults
Frequent Tripping of Circuit Breakers:
Possible Causes: Overloaded circuits, short circuits, or faulty wiring.
Diagnosis: Inspect circuit breakers for overloads or faults, and check wiring for damage or short circuits.
Inconsistent Power Supply:
Possible Causes: Loose connections, defective transformers, or power surges.
Diagnosis: Secure electrical connections, test transformers, and investigate potential power surges.
NonFunctional Thermostat:
Possible Causes: Dead batteries, wiring issues, or faulty thermostat.
Diagnosis: Replace batteries, check wiring connections, and test the thermostat for functionality.

Refrigerant Leaks
Symptoms of Leaks:
Low Cooling Efficiency: Reduced cooling performance or longer cooling cycles.
Frost or Ice Formation: Ice on evaporator coils or refrigerant lines.
Diagnosis:
Leak Detection: Use refrigerant leak detectors or soap solutions to identify leaks. Check connections and coils for signs of leakage.
Refrigerant Levels: Verify refrigerant levels and recharge as needed, addressing any leaks before recharging.

Airflow Problems
Drafts or Uneven Airflow:
Possible Causes: Leaky ductwork, poorly designed duct systems.
Diagnosis: Inspect and seal ductwork leaks, and evaluate duct design for proper airflow distribution.
Noise and Vibration Issues
Unusual Noises:
Possible Causes: Loose parts, worn bearings, or foreign objects.
Diagnosis: Identify the source of the noise, tighten loose parts, and remove any foreign objects.
Excessive Vibration:
Possible Causes: Imbalanced fans, misaligned components, or loose mounting.

Diagnosis: Balance fans, align components, and secure mounting to reduce vibration.

Chapter 16: Troubleshooting Methods

Diagnostic Techniques

Visual Inspection:

Steps: Begin with a thorough visual inspection of all HVAC components. Look for signs of wear, damage, or leakage. Check connections, wiring, and physical condition.

What to Look For: Discolored or burnt components, loose or disconnected wires, and signs of corrosion or rust.

Operational Testing:

Steps: Turn on the HVAC system and observe its operation. Listen for unusual noises and monitor system performance.

What to Check: Ensure the system starts up correctly, runs smoothly, and maintains the desired temperature.

System Isolation:

Steps: Isolate different components (e.g., heating vs. cooling) to determine which part of the system is malfunctioning.

Benefits: Helps pinpoint the exact location of the problem by narrowing down the potential sources.

Quick Fix Solutions

Resetting the System:

When to Use: If the system is not functioning correctly or displays error codes.

How to: Turn off the system, wait a few minutes, then turn it back on. This can sometimes clear minor issues.

Checking and Replacing Filters:

When to Use: If airflow is restricted or the system is not cooling or heating effectively.

How to: Inspect filters for dirt or clogs and replace them as needed to restore proper airflow.

Adjusting Thermostat Settings:

When to Use: If the temperature settings are not responding as expected.

How to: Verify and adjust thermostat settings to ensure they are correctly programmed for the desired temperature.

Inspecting and Clearing Drains:

When to Use: If there is water leakage or moisture around the system.

How to: Check and clear condensate drains to prevent blockages and ensure proper drainage.

Advanced Troubleshooting Procedures

Electrical System Analysis:

Steps: Use a multimeter to check for electrical continuity, voltage, and current in various components.

What to Check: Ensure all electrical components are functioning correctly and replace any faulty parts.

Refrigerant Pressure Testing:
Steps: Connect pressure gauges to the system and measure refrigerant pressures.
What to Check: Compare readings to manufacturer specifications and adjust refrigerant levels if necessary.

Component Testing:
Steps: Test individual components (e.g., compressors, capacitors) for proper operation.
What to Check: Verify that each component is working within its specified parameters.

Using Diagnostic Tools

Multimeter:
Purpose: Measures electrical parameters such as voltage, current, and resistance.
Usage: Used to diagnose electrical issues, test continuity, and check component functionality.

Manifold Gauge Set:
Purpose: Measures refrigerant pressure in HVAC systems.
Usage: Connect to service ports to assess refrigerant levels and diagnose cooling issues.

Thermometer:
Purpose: Measures temperature at various points in the system.
Usage: Used to check temperature differentials and diagnose heating or cooling problems.

Leak Detector:
Purpose: Detects refrigerant leaks in the system.
Usage: Use to identify and locate leaks, ensuring proper sealing and system performance.

Reading System Data and Logs

Understanding System Logs:
Steps: Access the system's data logs through the control panel or diagnostic software.
What to Look For: Review error codes, operational history, and performance metrics to identify issues.

Interpreting Error Codes:
Steps: Refer to the system's manual or manufacturer's documentation for error code meanings.
What to Check: Use error codes to guide troubleshooting efforts and address specific problems.

Analyzing Performance Data:
Steps: Review data on system performance, such as energy consumption and operational efficiency.
What to Check: Look for anomalies or deviations from normal performance that may indicate underlying issues.

Common Error Codes

Code Examples:
E1/E2: Sensor malfunctions or communication errors.
F1/F2: System overheating or low refrigerant issues.

P1/P2: Pressure switch problems or airflow issues.

Resolution Steps:

Steps: Refer to the error code list in the system manual and follow recommended troubleshooting steps.

What to Do: Address the specific issue indicated by the error code, such as replacing a faulty sensor or checking refrigerant levels.

Problem Resolution Strategies

StepbyStep Approach:

Steps: Follow a systematic approach to identify, diagnose, and resolve issues.

What to Do: Start with the most common problems and work through the troubleshooting steps until the issue is resolved.

Documentation and Review:

Steps: Document all findings, actions taken, and any parts replaced.

What to Do: Review the system's performance after repairs to ensure that the issue is fully resolved and no new problems have arisen.

Professional Assistance:

Steps: If troubleshooting does not resolve the issue, consult with a qualified HVAC technician.

What to Do: Provide detailed information about the problem and any diagnostic results to aid in further investigation.

Chapter 17: Professional Maintenance Services

When to Consult a Professional
Complex Issues:
Indicators: If you encounter problems that are beyond basic troubleshooting, such as electrical faults, refrigerant leaks, or complex system malfunctions.
Action: Consult a professional HVAC technician who has specialized knowledge and tools to diagnose and repair advanced issues.
System Overhaul or Major Repairs:
Indicators: When your HVAC system requires significant repairs or replacement of major components.
Action: Hire a professional to ensure proper installation or repair, adhering to manufacturer specifications and industry standards.
Regular Inspections and Maintenance:
Indicators: To keep your system in optimal condition, regular inspections and preventive maintenance are essential.
Action: Schedule routine visits with a professional to perform comprehensive checks and maintenance tasks.
Compliance with Regulations:
Indicators: When your system needs to meet local building codes or safety regulations.
Action: Engage a certified professional to ensure compliance with all applicable laws and standards.
Service Contracts and Agreements
Types of Service Contracts:
Preventive Maintenance Contracts: Regular inspections and maintenance services are scheduled at set intervals.
FullService Contracts: Comprehensive coverage including repairs, parts replacement, and emergency services.
Custom Agreements: Tailored contracts based on specific needs and system requirements.
Benefits of Service Contracts:
Cost Savings: Reduced costs for repairs and maintenance through fixed monthly or annual fees.
Priority Service: Faster response times and priority scheduling for service requests.
Scheduled Maintenance: Regular upkeep helps prevent unexpected breakdowns and extends the lifespan of your HVAC system.
Selecting a Contract:
Considerations: Evaluate the scope of services, coverage limits, and costs associated with different contract options.
Action: Choose a contract that aligns with your system's needs and your budget, ensuring comprehensive coverage.

Maintenance Management Software

Features and Benefits:

Scheduling: Automated reminders for scheduled maintenance and inspections.

Tracking: Monitoring system performance, maintenance history, and repair records.

Reporting: Generating detailed reports on service activities and system status.

Popular Software Options:

Examples: Software like ServiceTitan, Facilio, or CMMS (Computerized Maintenance Management System) tools.

Comparison: Evaluate features, ease of use, and integration capabilities to select the most suitable software for your needs.

Implementation Tips:

Integration: Ensure the software integrates with existing systems and workflows.

Training: Provide staff training to effectively use the software and leverage its features.

Choosing a Service Provider

Qualifications and Certification:

What to Look For: Ensure the provider has relevant certifications (e.g., NATE, EPA) and licensed technicians.

Why It Matters: Certifications and licenses indicate a provider's expertise and adherence to industry standards.

Reputation and Reviews:

What to Check: Read customer reviews, check ratings, and ask for references from previous clients.

Why It Matters: Positive feedback and a strong reputation reflect reliable and high-quality service.

Experience and Specialization:

What to Look For: Choose a provider with experience in servicing your specific type of HVAC system and expertise in relevant technologies.

Why It Matters: Specialized knowledge ensures accurate diagnosis and effective solutions for your system.

Cost and Transparency:

What to Evaluate: Obtain detailed quotes and ensure there are no hidden fees or charges.

Why It Matters: Transparent pricing helps you make informed decisions and avoid unexpected costs.

Cost Benefit Analysis

Analyzing Costs:

Factors: Consider initial investment, ongoing maintenance costs, and potential repair expenses.

Calculation: Compare costs with expected savings from improved system efficiency and reduced breakdowns.

Evaluating Benefits:
Factors: Assess benefits such as increased system longevity, enhanced performance, and lower energy bills.
Impact: Determine how the investment in maintenance services contributes to overall savings and system reliability.

Enhancing Service Quality

Training and Certification:
Focus: Ensure technicians receive ongoing training and certification to stay updated with industry advancements.
Benefit: Well-trained technicians provide higher quality service and more effective solutions.

Customer Communication:
Focus: Maintain clear and open communication with customers regarding service plans, repair progress, and recommendations.
Benefit: Good communication fosters trust and ensures customers are well-informed about their system's status.

Quality Assurance:
Focus: Implement quality control measures to monitor and improve service standards.
Benefit: Regular audits and feedback collection help maintain high service quality and customer satisfaction.

Customer Satisfaction

Feedback and Reviews:
Focus: Encourage customers to provide feedback and leave reviews after service.
Benefit: Feedback helps identify areas for improvement and build a positive reputation.

Responsive Service:
Focus: Provide prompt and efficient responses to service requests and inquiries.
Benefit: Quick response times enhance customer satisfaction and build trust.

FollowUp:
Focus: Conduct follow-up calls or surveys to ensure customers are satisfied with the service provided.
Benefit: Followups demonstrate commitment to customer satisfaction and provide opportunities for addressing any additional concerns.

Book 5

Essential HVAC Tools and Equipment

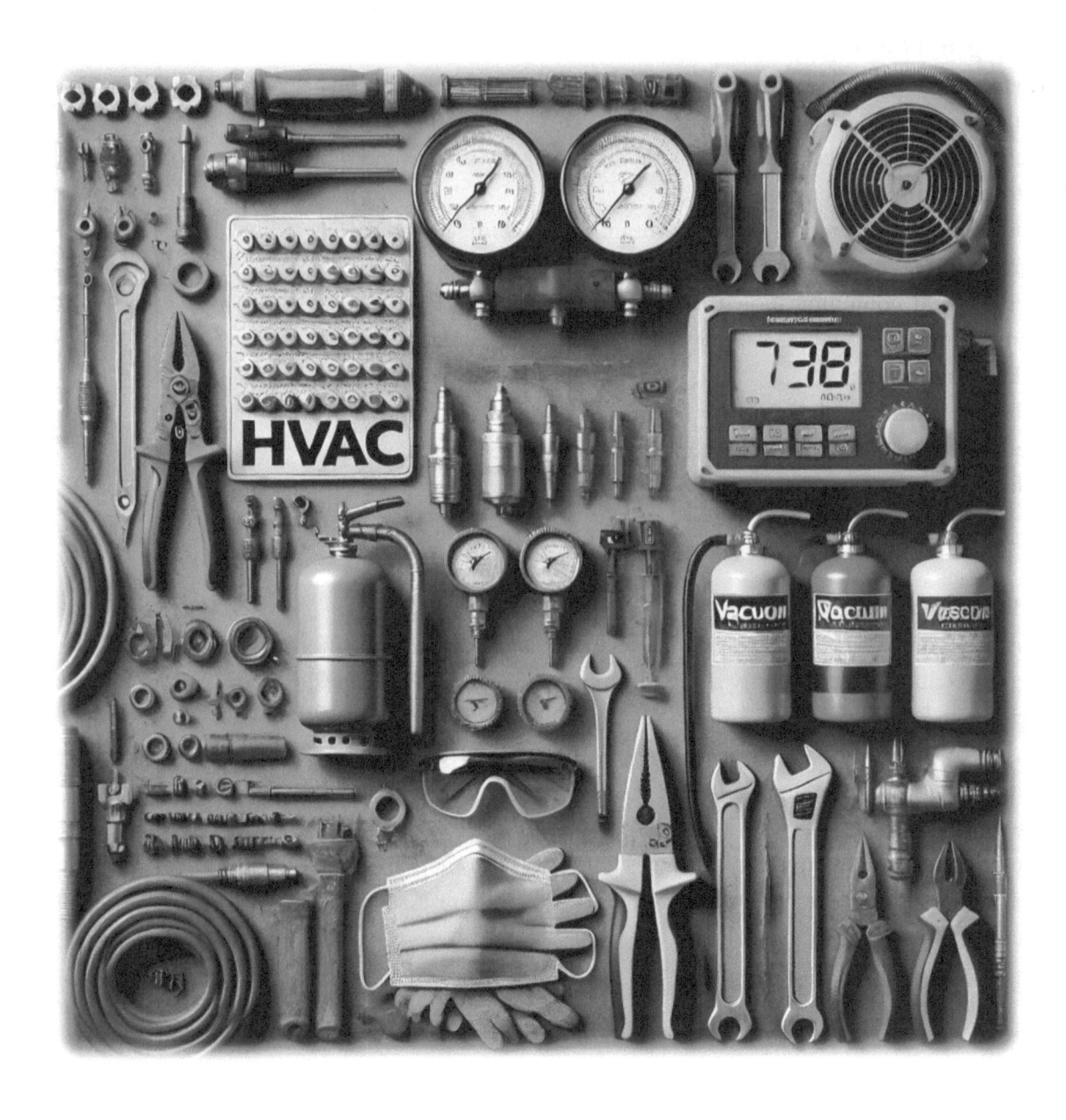

Chapter 18: Basic HVAC Tools

Hand Tools Overview
Screwdrivers:
Types: Flathead, Phillips, Torx, and specialty screwdrivers.
Uses: Essential for tightening or loosening screws on HVAC components. Choose ergonomic handles for comfort and efficiency.
Pliers:
Types: Needlenose, slip joint, and lineman's pliers.
Uses: Used for gripping, bending, and cutting wires or metal parts. Needlenose pliers are ideal for precision work in tight spaces.
Wrenches:
Types: Adjustable, combination, and socket wrenches.
Uses: Vital for turning nuts and bolts. Adjustable wrenches are versatile, while socket wrenches offer quick changes between sizes.
Hammers and Mallets:
Types: Claw hammers, sledgehammers, and rubber mallets.
Uses: Hammers are used for driving nails or breaking components, while mallets prevent damage to delicate surfaces.

Measuring Instruments
Thermometers:
Types: Digital, infrared, and dial thermometers.
Uses: Measure temperatures of air, refrigerants, and components to ensure they are operating within specified ranges.
Manifold Gauges:
Types: Analog and digital manifold gauge sets.
Uses: Measure refrigerant pressure in the system, essential for diagnosing cooling issues and ensuring proper refrigerant levels.
Multimeter:
Types: Digital and analog multimeters.
Uses: Measure electrical parameters such as voltage, current, and resistance. Crucial for diagnosing electrical issues and ensuring safe operation.
Manometer:
Types: Digital and analog manometers.
Uses: Measure pressure in various components, including gas lines and air ducts, to ensure systems operate efficiently and safely.

Specialized HVAC ToolsRefrigerant Leak Detectors:

Types: Electronic, ultrasonic, and halide leak detectors.

Uses: Identify and locate refrigerant leaks, ensuring system efficiency and preventing environmental damage.

Vacuum Pumps:

Types: Single-stage and two-stage vacuum pumps.

Uses: Remove air and moisture from the refrigeration system before charging it with refrigerant.

Duct Cleaners:

Types: Rotary brushes and airpowered cleaners.

Uses: Clean and maintain air ducts, ensuring proper airflow and indoor air quality.

Borescopes:

Types: Digital and analog borescopes.

Uses: Inspect hard-to-reach areas within HVAC systems, such as inside ducts or behind components.

Tool Kits for Technicians

Basic Technician Kit:

Contents: Screwdrivers, pliers, wrenches, multimeters, and a few specialized tools like a refrigerant gauge set.

Uses: Provides essential tools for everyday HVAC tasks and basic troubleshooting.

Advanced Technician Kit:

Contents: Includes all items from the basic kit plus additional tools like vacuum pumps, leak detectors, and borescopes.

Uses: Ideal for more complex installations, repairs, and diagnostics.

Portable Tool Kits:

Contents: Compact and organized kits with essential tools for mobile technicians.

Uses: Designed for convenience and ease of transport, allowing technicians to perform tasks on-site efficiently.

Essential Tools for DIY

Basic Hand Tools:

Contents: Screwdrivers, pliers, wrenches, and hammers.

Uses: Suitable for simple repairs and maintenance tasks around the home.

Basic Measuring Instruments:

Contents: Digital thermometer and basic multimeter.

Uses: Allows homeowners to check temperatures and electrical parameters.

Safety Tools:

Contents: Safety glasses, gloves, and a flashlight.

Uses: Ensures safety during DIY repairs and maintenance.

Safety Tools and Gear

Personal Protective Equipment (PPE):

Types: Safety goggles, gloves, and hearing protection.
Uses: Protects against injury and exposure to hazardous materials during HVAC work.
Fall Protection Gear:
Types: Harnesses, lanyards, and safety belts.
Uses: Essential for working at heights or on roofs to prevent falls.
Respiratory Protection:
Types: Dust masks and respirators.
Uses: Protects against inhaling dust, fumes, or refrigerants during maintenance tasks.

Tool Selection Criteria

Quality and Durability:
Considerations: Choose tools made from high-quality materials that offer durability and long service life.
Why It Matters: High-quality tools withstand heavy use and provide reliable performance.
Ergonomics and Comfort:
Considerations: Select tools with comfortable grips and ergonomic designs to reduce fatigue and improve efficiency.
Why It Matters: Ergonomic tools enhance productivity and minimize strain during use.
Accuracy and Precision:
Considerations: Ensure measuring instruments and specialized tools offer accurate readings and precise results.
Why It Matters: Accurate tools contribute to effective diagnostics and proper system adjustments.
Versatility and Functionality:
Considerations: Choose tools that offer multiple functions or are compatible with a range of HVAC systems and components.
Why It Matters: Versatile tools provide more value and flexibility for various tasks.
Cost and Budget:
Considerations: Balance tool costs with quality and features, considering both initial investment and long-term value.
Why It Matters: Invest in tools that offer the best performance within your budget constraints.

Chapter 19: Advanced HVAC Tools

Electrical Testing Instruments
Multimeters:

Description: Versatile instruments for measuring electrical parameters such as voltage, current, and resistance.

Applications: Troubleshooting electrical issues, checking continuity, and verifying circuit integrity.

Features to Consider: Digital display, auto-ranging capability, and safety ratings.

Clamp Meters:

Description: Tools used to measure current without disconnecting the circuit.

Applications: Measuring current in live wires and diagnosing electrical faults.

Features to Consider: Accurate current measurement, ease of use, and additional functions like voltage and resistance measurement.

Voltage Testers:

Description: Simple tools for checking the presence of voltage.

Applications: Ensuring electrical circuits are de-energized before working on them.

Features to Consider: Visual and audible indicators, reliability, and ease of handling.

Tools for Handling Refrigerants
Refrigerant Recovery Machines:

Description: Machines designed to recover refrigerants during system maintenance or repair.

Applications: Safe recovery and recycling of refrigerants, complying with environmental regulations.

Features to Consider: Recovery speed, refrigerant compatibility, and ease of use.

Charging Scales:

Description: Scales are used to measure the amount of refrigerant being added to or removed from a system.

Applications: Ensuring accurate refrigerant charges and maintaining system efficiency.

Features to Consider: Precision, capacity, and digital readout.

Refrigerant Leak Detectors:

Description: Tools specifically designed to detect refrigerant leaks.

Types: Electronic, ultrasonic, and halide torch.

Applications: Identifying leaks in HVAC systems to prevent refrigerant loss and system damage.

Features to Consider: Sensitivity, detection range, and ease of calibration.

Combustion Analysis Tools
Combustion Analyzers:

Description: Instruments used to measure the efficiency and emissions of combustion appliances.

Applications: Evaluating furnace, boiler, and water heater performance.

Features to Consider: Measurement accuracy, ease of use, and capability to analyze multiple gases.

Draft Gauges:

Description: Tools for measuring draft pressure in combustion systems.

Applications: Ensuring proper draft in flues and vents to prevent backdrafts and ensure efficient combustion.

Features to Consider: Sensitivity, range, and ease of calibration.

Digital Manifolds:

Description: Advanced manifold gauges with digital displays for accurate refrigerant pressure measurements.

Applications: Diagnosing refrigerant system performance and managing refrigerant charges.

Features to Consider: Digital readouts, real-time pressure readings, and built-in diagnostic functions.

Ultrasonic Leak Detectors:

Description: Devices that detect leaks by picking up high-frequency sound waves produced by escaping gases or liquids.

Applications: Identifying leaks in noisy environments where other methods might be ineffective.

Features to Consider: Sensitivity, range, and ease of use in various conditions.

Infrared Cameras:

Description: Cameras that capture thermal images to detect heat patterns and anomalies in HVAC systems.

Applications: Identifying insulation problems, detecting electrical hot spots, and locating air leaks.

Features to Consider: Image resolution, temperature range, and ease of use.

Specialty Tools for Advanced Systems

Vibration Analyzers:

Description: Instruments used to measure vibrations and diagnose mechanical issues in HVAC equipment.

Applications: Identifying imbalances, misalignments, and wear in motors and fans.

Features to Consider: Sensitivity, range, and data analysis capabilities.

Airflow Balancing Tools:

Description: Tools used to measure and adjust airflow in HVAC systems to ensure proper distribution.

Applications: Balancing air distribution in complex duct systems and optimizing system performance.

Features to Consider: Accuracy, ease of adjustment, and compatibility with various systems.

Duct Leak Detectors:

Description: Tools designed to identify leaks in ductwork.

Applications: Ensuring duct systems are sealed properly to improve system efficiency and indoor air quality.

Features to Consider: Sensitivity, ease of use, and data recording capabilities.

Chapter 20: Maintaining Your Tools

Cleaning and Storing Tools
Cleaning Procedures:
Description: Regular cleaning to ensure tools remain in optimal condition and function properly.
General Guidelines:
Hand Tools: Wipe off dirt and grime with a damp cloth; for stubborn residue, use a mild detergent and brush.
Precision Instruments: Use manufacturer-recommended cleaning agents to avoid damaging sensitive components.
Refrigerant Tools: Clean after use to remove refrigerant residues and dirt; follow safety protocols for handling chemicals.
Storage Practices:
Description: Proper storage prevents damage and prolongs tool lifespan.
General Guidelines:
Tool Boxes and Racks: Store tools in designated toolboxes or racks to avoid rust and damage.
Climate-Controlled Storage: For sensitive instruments, use climate-controlled environments to prevent moisture and temperature-related issues.
Protective Covers: Use covers or cases to shield tools from dust and accidental damage.

Calibration Techniques
Why Calibration is Important:
Description: Calibration ensures tools provide accurate and reliable measurements.
Applications: Essential for measurement tools like multimeters, pressure gauges, and thermometers.
Calibration Procedures:
Digital Thermometers: Calibrate using known temperature standards and adjust settings as needed.
Manifold Gauges: Use calibration kits to adjust pressure readings and verify accuracy.
Refrigerant Scales: Calibrate with certified weights to ensure precise measurements.
Frequency of Calibration:
Description: Regular calibration is crucial for maintaining accuracy.
General Guidelines: Follow manufacturer recommendations for calibration intervals, typically every 6 to 12 months or before critical measurements.

Performing Safety Checks
Inspection Guidelines:
Description: Regular inspections to identify potential hazards and ensure safe operation.
General Guidelines:
Visual Checks: Inspect tools for visible damage such as cracks, rust, or wear.

Functional Tests: Verify that tools operate correctly and safely before each use.
Electrical Safety: For electrical tools, check cords and plugs for damage and ensure proper grounding.
Safety Protocols:
Description: Implement safety protocols to prevent accidents and injuries.
General Guidelines: Follow safety instructions provided by the tool manufacturer and adhere to standard operating procedures.

Repair and Replacement
Repair Procedures:
Description: Addressing minor issues to extend tool lifespan and maintain functionality.
General Guidelines:
Minor Repairs: Replace worn-out parts like handles, blades, or batteries.
Professional Repairs: For complex issues, seek professional repair services or consult the manufacturer.
Replacement Guidelines:
Description: When to replace tools versus repairing them.
General Guidelines:
Cost Benefit Analysis: Compare the cost of repairs to the cost of replacement.
Tool Condition: Replace tools that are beyond repair or have reached the end of their useful life.

Tool Inventory Management
Inventory Tracking:
Description: Keeping an organized record of tools to manage availability and prevent loss.
General Guidelines:
Inventory Systems: Use software or spreadsheets to track tool locations, conditions, and maintenance schedules.
Regular Audits: Conduct periodic inventory audits to ensure all tools are accounted for and in good condition.
Procurement and Replacement:
Description: Managing tool acquisition and replacement to meet operational needs.
General Guidelines:
Tool Requests: Implement a system for requesting and ordering new tools as needed.
Budget Management: Allocate funds for tool procurement and replacement within the budget.

Tool Lifespan and Usage
Understanding Tool Lifespan:
Description: Knowing the expected lifespan of tools helps in planning for replacements and maintenance.

General Guidelines: Refer to manufacturer guidelines and industry standards for expected tool lifespans.

Optimizing Tool Usage:

Description: Using tools efficiently to extend their lifespan and maintain performance.

General Guidelines:

Proper Use: Follow manufacturer recommendations for usage to prevent excessive wear and tear.

Maintenance: Regular maintenance helps keep tools in good working order and extends their lifespan.

Cost Effective Tool Maintenance

Preventive Maintenance:

Description: Routine maintenance practices that help prevent tool breakdowns and costly repairs.

General Guidelines: Implement regular cleaning, calibration, and safety checks to minimize unexpected repairs.

Budget Friendly Maintenance:

Description: Cost-effective strategies for maintaining tools without overspending.

General Guidelines:

DIY Maintenance: Perform simple maintenance tasks in-house to save on professional service costs.

Bulk Purchases: Buy maintenance supplies in bulk to reduce costs.

Long Term Planning:

Description: Planning for tool maintenance and replacement to manage costs effectively.

General Guidelines: Develop a maintenance schedule and budget for tool replacements to avoid unexpected expenses.

Chapter 21: Safety Equipment

Protective Gear

Description: Essential gear to protect HVAC technicians from various hazards encountered on the job.

Purpose: Ensure personal safety and reduce the risk of injuries and exposure to harmful substances.

Types of Protective Gear:

Safety Helmets: Protects the head from falling objects and impacts. Ensure proper fit and compliance with safety standards.

Eye Protection: Safety goggles or face shields guard against flying debris, chemicals, and intense light. Choose appropriate lenses based on the specific job requirements.

Hearing Protection: Earplugs or earmuffs to reduce exposure to high noise levels that can cause hearing damage. Select based on noise reduction rating (NRR) and comfort.

Gloves: Various types for different tasks, including cut-resistant, chemical-resistant, and insulated gloves. Ensure gloves fit well and are appropriate for the job.

Safety Protocols

Description: Procedures and guidelines designed to ensure a safe working environment and minimize risks.

Purpose: Promote safe work practices and prevent accidents.

General Protocols:

PreWork Safety Checks: Inspect tools, equipment, and work areas for potential hazards before starting work.

Hazard Communication: Identify and communicate potential hazards related to specific tasks or environments.

Emergency Procedures: Know and practice emergency response procedures for situations such as fires, chemical spills, or electrical hazards.

Specific Protocols:

Lockout/Tagout (LOTO): Implement procedures to ensure machinery is properly shut off and cannot be accidentally turned on during maintenance.

Confined Space Entry: Follow guidelines for entering and working in confined spaces, including ventilation and atmospheric testing.

Personal Protective Equipment (PPE)

Description: Equipment worn to protect against various hazards encountered during HVAC work.

Purpose: Safeguard against injuries and health risks.

Types of PPE:

Respirators: Protect against inhaling harmful substances such as dust, fumes, and chemicals. Choose appropriate types (e.g., N95 masks, full-face respirators) based on the specific hazards.

Fall Protection: Harnesses, lanyards, and anchor points to prevent falls from heights. Ensure proper use and regular inspection.

Work Boots: Safety boots with steel toes and slip-resistant soles to protect feet from impacts and slips. Ensure proper fit and comfort.

Emergency Response Equipment

Description: Equipment used to respond to emergencies and provide first aid.

Purpose: Quickly address and manage emergencies to prevent injuries and mitigate damage.

Types of Emergency Response Equipment:

First Aid Kits: Comprehensive kits containing supplies for treating minor injuries, including bandages, antiseptics, and splints. Regularly check and replenish supplies.

Fire Extinguishers: Equipment for extinguishing small fires. Choose the appropriate type (e.g., ABC, CO2) based on potential fire hazards.

Emergency Eyewash Stations: Installed in areas where chemicals or debris may come into contact with the eyes. Ensure accessibility and functionality.

Safe Work Practices

Description: Procedures and behaviors designed to maintain safety while performing HVAC tasks.

Purpose: Reduce the risk of accidents and ensure a safe working environment.

Examples of Safe Work Practices:

Proper Lifting Techniques: Use correct body mechanics to lift heavy objects and avoid back injuries.

Use of Tools and Equipment: Operate tools and equipment according to manufacturer instructions and safety guidelines.

Housekeeping: Keep work areas clean and free of clutter to prevent trips and falls.

Safety Training and Certification

Description: Training programs and certifications that enhance safety knowledge and skills.

Purpose: Ensure technicians are well informed and capable of handling safety-related aspects of their work.

Types of Training and Certification:

OSHA Certification: Training on workplace safety standards and regulations set by the Occupational Safety and Health Administration (OSHA).

Hazardous Materials Training: Education on handling and working with hazardous materials, including proper storage and disposal.

First Aid and CPR Certification: Training on providing first aid and performing cardiopulmonary resuscitation (CPR) in emergencies.

Regulatory Compliance

Description: Adherence to laws, regulations, and industry standards related to safety and health.

Purpose: Ensure compliance with legal requirements and maintain a safe working environment.

Key Regulations:

OSHA Standards: Compliance with OSHA regulations regarding workplace safety, including personal protective equipment and safety protocols.

Environmental Regulations: Adherence to regulations concerning the handling and disposal of hazardous materials, such as refrigerants.

Industry Standards: Follow industry-specific standards for safety practices, tool use, and equipment maintenance.

Book 6

Designing and Planning HVAC Systems

Chapter 22: Calculating Loads

Manual J and Load Calculations

Description: Manual J is a standard methodology for calculating the heating and cooling loads of residential buildings.

Purpose: Ensure accurate sizing of HVAC systems to meet the specific needs of a building.

Manual J Calculation Process:

Data Collection: Gather information about the building's size, construction materials, windows, doors, insulation, and occupancy.

Heat Gain and Loss: Calculate the amount of heat gained from external sources (e.g., sunlight) and lost through walls, windows, and ceilings.

Equipment Sizing: Use the calculated loads to determine the appropriate size and capacity of HVAC equipment.

Tools and Resources:

Manual J Software: Use specialized software tools designed to simplify the calculation process and ensure accuracy.

Understanding Heat Gain and Loss

Description: Heat gain and loss are critical factors in determining the HVAC system's capacity requirements.

Purpose: Assess how external and internal factors affect the temperature and comfort levels within a building.

Heat Gain:

Sources: Solar radiation, lighting, appliances, and occupants contribute to heat gain.

Calculation Methods: Evaluate heat gain through windows, walls, roofs, and other components using formulas and software tools.

Heat Loss:

Sources: Heat loss occurs through conduction, convection, and radiation through building envelopes.

Calculation Methods: Measure heat loss through walls, windows, and roofs, considering factors such as insulation levels and outdoor temperatures.

Software Tools for Load Calculation

Description: Software tools assist in performing complex load calculations efficiently and accurately.

Purpose: Streamline the calculation process and reduce the risk of errors.

Popular Software Tools:

HVAC Load Explorer: Provides detailed load calculations and system sizing recommendations.

Cool Calc: An online tool for performing Manual J load calculations and generating reports.

Energy Star Portfolio Manager: Offers energy performance tracking and load analysis features.

Benefits:

Accuracy: Improve precision in load calculations compared to manual methods.

Efficiency: Save time and effort by automating complex calculations.

Residential vs. Commercial Loads

Description: Load calculation methods and requirements differ between residential and commercial buildings.

Purpose: Tailor HVAC system designs to meet the specific needs of different building types.

Residential Loads:

Characteristics: Generally involve smaller spaces, fewer occupants, and lower heat gain from commercial activities.

Calculation Considerations: Focus on factors such as family size, usage patterns, and building orientation.

Commercial Loads:

Characteristics: Larger spaces, higher occupancy levels, and significant heat gain from equipment and lighting.

Calculation Considerations: Include factors such as equipment heat load, lighting intensity, and variable occupancy.

Seasonal Variations

Description: Seasonal changes impact heating and cooling loads, affecting HVAC system performance.

Purpose: Adjust load calculations to account for variations in outdoor temperatures and building usage throughout the year.

Winter and Summer Loads:

Winter: Calculate heating loads considering outdoor temperatures, wind chill, and building insulation.

Summer: Determine cooling loads based on outdoor temperatures, solar gain, and internal heat sources.

Impact of Seasonal Variations:

System Sizing: Ensure HVAC systems are sized to handle peak load conditions in both winter and summer.

Efficiency: Optimize system performance and energy efficiency by accounting for seasonal variations in load calculations.

Load Calculation Case Studies

Description: Real-world examples demonstrate the application of load calculation methods in different scenarios.

Purpose: Provide practical insights into the challenges and solutions in HVAC system design.

Case Study Examples:
Residential Home: Analyze load calculations for a typical single-family home, considering factors such as size, insulation, and occupancy.
Commercial Office Building: Examine load calculations for a multistory office building, including considerations for equipment, lighting, and occupancy patterns.
Lessons Learned:
Accuracy: Emphasize the importance of accurate data collection and calculation methods.
Customization: Highlight the need for tailored solutions based on specific building characteristics and usage patterns.

Impact of Building Envelopes

Description: The building envelope plays a crucial role in determining heating and cooling loads.
Purpose: Assess how building materials, insulation, and design affect HVAC system performance.
Components of Building Envelopes:
Walls: Consider the type of materials, insulation levels, and thermal resistance.
Windows: Evaluate the impact of window size, type, and shading on heat gain and loss.
Roofs: Analyze roof materials, insulation, and ventilation to determine their effect on load calculations.
Influence on Load Calculations:
Heat Transfer: Understand how building envelopes affect heat transfer between indoor and outdoor environments.
Energy Efficiency: Optimize building envelope design to improve energy efficiency and reduce HVAC system loads.

Chapter 23: Designing Ductwork

Sizing and Layout Planning

Description: Proper ductwork design is crucial for efficient HVAC system performance. Sizing and layout planning ensure optimal airflow and system efficiency.

Purpose: Create a duct system that balances airflow, minimizes energy loss, and meets the heating and cooling needs of the building.

Duct Sizing:

Calculation Methods: Use Manual D or other duct sizing methods to determine the appropriate duct dimensions based on airflow requirements.

Tools: Utilize duct sizing calculators and software to simplify the process and ensure accuracy.

Layout Planning:

Design Considerations: Plan ductwork routes to minimize bends, transitions, and restrictions. Ensure that ducts are routed efficiently and unobtrusively throughout the building.

Space Allocation: Allocate adequate space for ductwork within ceilings, walls, and floors to avoid conflicts with other building systems.

Best Practices:

Minimize Length: Keep duct runs as short as possible to reduce energy losses and improve system efficiency.

Avoid Sharp Turns: Use gradual bends and wide-radius elbows to maintain smooth airflow and reduce pressure drops.

Material Selection Criteria

Description: Choosing the right materials for ductwork is essential for durability, performance, and energy efficiency.

Purpose: Select materials that meet the specific needs of the HVAC system and building environment.

Common Materials:

Sheet Metal: Durable and commonly used for ductwork. Galvanized steel is a popular choice due to its corrosion resistance.

Flexible Ducts: Made of plastic and metal, suitable for tight spaces and easy installation. Ensure they are properly supported to prevent sagging.

Fiberglass Duct Board: Provides good insulation properties and noise reduction but can be prone to damage.

Selection Factors:

Durability: Consider the material's resistance to wear, corrosion, and damage.

Insulation: Choose materials with adequate insulation properties to reduce heat loss or gain.

Cost: Balance material costs with performance and longevity to achieve cost-effective solutions.

Duct Insulation Methods

Description: Insulating ductwork helps maintain the temperature of the air within the ducts and improves system efficiency.

Purpose: Reduce energy loss, prevent condensation, and enhance comfort.

Insulation Materials:

Fiberglass Insulation: Commonly used for its thermal resistance and soundproofing qualities. Apply it around the exterior of the ducts.

Foam Insulation: Provides high insulation value and is used in preinsulated ducts or as a coating.

Reflective Insulation: Features a reflective surface to reduce heat gain or loss.

Installation Techniques:

Wrap Insulation: Wrap ducts with fiberglass or foam insulation and secure them with tape or bands.

Foam Coating: Apply spray foam insulation to ducts for a seamless, high-efficiency solution.

Proper Sealing: Ensure all insulation is properly sealed to prevent air leaks and maintain effectiveness.

Airflow Calculations

Description: Accurate airflow calculations ensure that the ductwork delivers the right amount of air to each space, promoting even temperature distribution and comfort.

Purpose: Design ducts to handle the required airflow without excessive pressure drops or noise.

Calculation Methods:

CFM Requirements: Calculate cubic feet per minute (CFM) requirements for each room based on its size and usage.

Velocity and Pressure: Use velocity and pressure formulas to determine duct sizes and minimize pressure losses.

Tools:

Airflow Calculators: Use specialized software and calculators to perform airflow calculations efficiently.

Manometers and Anemometers: Measure static pressure and airflow velocity during system testing.

Pressure Balancing

Description: Proper pressure balancing ensures that all areas of the building receive adequate airflow and prevents pressure imbalances that can affect system performance.

Purpose: Achieve balanced air distribution and avoid issues such as drafts or hot and cold spots.

Balancing Techniques:

Manual Dampers: Adjust manual dampers in ducts to regulate airflow to different areas.

Airflow Balancing Devices: Use balancing devices such as flow hoods or dampers to finetune airflow and pressure.

Best Practices:

Regular Testing: Perform pressure tests and adjustments during and after installation to ensure proper balance.

System Adjustments: Make necessary adjustments based on test results and feedback from building occupants.

Noise Control Techniques

Description: Reducing noise in ductwork improves comfort and minimizes disruptions in living or working environments.

Purpose: Achieve quieter HVAC operation and enhance overall satisfaction.

Noise Reduction Methods:

Acoustic Duct Linings: Install acoustic liners inside ducts to absorb sound and reduce noise.

Flexible Ducts: Use flexible ducts with sound-absorbing materials to minimize noise transmission.

Vibration Isolation: Apply vibration isolators to duct connections and equipment to reduce noise from mechanical vibrations.

Design Considerations:

Duct Size and Shape: Design ducts with appropriate sizes and shapes to minimize turbulence and noise.

Sound Attenuators: Install sound attenuators in duct systems to further reduce noise levels.

Custom Ductwork Solutions

Description: Custom ductwork solutions address unique design challenges and requirements, providing tailored solutions for specific building needs.

Purpose: Ensure optimal performance and integration with building designs.

Custom Design Approaches:

Bespoke Duct Designs: Create custom ductwork designs for complex layouts or architectural features.

Fabrication Services: Use specialized fabrication services to produce custom ductwork components.

Examples and Case Studies:

Historical Buildings: Design and install custom ductwork solutions for historical or landmark buildings while preserving architectural integrity.

Commercial Spaces: Develop custom duct systems for large commercial spaces with unique heating and cooling needs.

Chapter 24: Implementing System Zoning

Benefits of Zoning

Description: System zoning divides a building into distinct areas, each with its temperature control, enhancing comfort and energy efficiency.

Purpose: Optimize heating and cooling to meet the specific needs of different areas within a building.

Comfort:

Personalized Control: Allows occupants to set different temperatures for various zones, accommodating individual preferences.

Reduced Temperature Fluctuations: Minimizes the impact of temperature changes in one zone on others.

Energy Efficiency:

Targeted Heating/Cooling: Reduces energy use by heating or cooling only the areas in use, rather than the entire building.

Cost Savings: Lowers utility bills by avoiding overconditioning unused spaces.

Enhanced System Performance:

Improved Air Distribution: Balances airflow and temperature across different zones for more efficient system operation.

Reduced Wear and Tear: Lessens the strain on HVAC equipment by avoiding constant load operation.

Zoning System Implementation

Description: Implementing a zoning system involves installing controls and ductwork that enable independent temperature regulation for different areas.

Purpose: Ensure effective and efficient zoning that meets the building's comfort and efficiency goals.

Planning:

Assessment: Evaluate the building layout, occupancy patterns, and specific heating/cooling needs to determine zoning requirements.

Design: Create a detailed plan for the zoning system, including ductwork modifications, control placement, and sensor locations.

Installation:

Zoning Dampers: Install motorized dampers in ductwork to control airflow to different zones.

Thermostats and Controls: Set up programmable or smart thermostats for each zone to manage temperature settings independently.

Wiring and Connectivity: Ensure proper wiring and integration of controls and sensors with the HVAC system.

Testing:

System Verification: Test the zoning system to verify proper operation and make necessary adjustments for optimal performance.

Calibration: Calibrate thermostats and sensors to ensure accurate temperature readings and control.

Zoning Control Solutions

Description: Control solutions for zoning systems allow for precise management of temperature settings and system operation.

Purpose: Provide flexibility and efficiency in managing different zones within a building.

Thermostats:

Programmable Thermostats: Allow users to set specific schedules for heating and cooling in each zone.

Smart Thermostats: Offer advanced features such as remote control, learning algorithms, and integration with smart home systems.

Control Panels:

Zoning Control Panels: Centralize the management of multiple zones, enabling easy adjustments and monitoring.

User Interfaces: Provide intuitive interfaces for setting temperature schedules and viewing system status.

Sensors:

Temperature Sensors: Monitor and provide feedback on the temperature in each zone, ensuring accurate control.

Occupancy Sensors: Adjust heating and cooling based on room occupancy to enhance efficiency.

Zone Design Considerations

Description: Effective zone design involves considering factors that impact the performance and efficiency of the zoning system.

Purpose: Create a well-balanced and functional zoning system that meets the building's needs.

Building Layout:

Room Usage: Design zones based on the purpose and usage patterns of different rooms or areas.

Heat Sources: Account for internal heat sources such as appliances and lighting when designing zones.

Ductwork and Airflow:

Duct Sizing: Ensure that ductwork is properly sized and balanced to deliver adequate airflow to each zone.

Airflow Distribution: Design duct layouts to avoid airflow imbalances and ensure even temperature distribution.

Insulation and Sealing:

Duct Insulation: Insulate ductwork to prevent heat loss or gain and maintain energy efficiency.

Sealing: Seal all duct connections and joints to prevent air leaks and ensure system performance.

Zoning for Energy Efficiency

Description: Implementing zoning strategies to enhance energy efficiency can lead to significant cost savings and reduced environmental impact.

Purpose: Maximize the benefits of zoning by optimizing energy use.

EnergyEfficient Practices:

Setback Strategies: Use zoning to implement setback temperatures during periods of low occupancy.

Load Management: Adjust heating and cooling based on real-time load conditions and occupancy data.

Integration with Smart Systems:

Smart Controls: Integrate zoning with smart home systems to automate temperature adjustments based on occupancy and weather conditions.

Energy Monitoring: Use energy monitoring tools to track and analyze energy consumption patterns.

Zoning System Maintenance

Description: Regular maintenance is essential to ensure the continued efficiency and performance of zoning systems.

Purpose: Maintain optimal system operation and prevent potential issues.

Routine Checks:

System Inspection: Perform regular inspections of zoning controls, thermostats, and dampers.

Cleaning: Clean filters, sensors, and other components to ensure proper function.

Adjustments and Calibration:

Thermostat Calibration: Recalibrate thermostats and sensors as needed to maintain accurate temperature control.

Damper Adjustments: Adjust zoning dampers to address any changes in airflow or temperature distribution.

Case Studies in Zoning

Description: Case studies illustrate the practical application of zoning systems and their benefits in real-world scenarios.

Purpose: Provide insights and lessons learned from successful zoning implementations.

Residential Case Studies:

Example: A residential home with multiple zones for different family members and areas, demonstrating improved comfort and energy savings.

Lessons Learned: Insights into effective zoning design and common challenges.

Commercial Case Studies:

Example: A commercial building with zoning for different office spaces and meeting rooms, showcasing enhanced efficiency and occupant satisfaction.

Lessons Learned: Best practices for managing zoning in commercial settings and addressing unique requirements.

Chapter 25: Enhancing Energy Efficiency

SEER Ratings and Their Importance
Understanding SEER Ratings:

Definition: SEER (Seasonal Energy Efficiency Ratio) measures the cooling efficiency of air conditioners and heat pumps over an entire cooling season. It is calculated by dividing the total cooling output (in BTUs) by the total energy consumed (in watt-hours).

Importance: A higher SEER rating indicates greater efficiency and lower energy consumption. For example, a unit with a SEER rating of 16 is more efficient than one with a rating of 14, leading to lower operating costs.

Impact on Energy Consumption:

Cost Savings: Higher SEERrated units reduce monthly energy bills by using less electricity to achieve the same level of cooling.

Environmental Benefits: Improved efficiency lowers the carbon footprint, contributing to environmental conservation by reducing greenhouse gas emissions.

Choosing the Right SEER Rating:

Climate Considerations: In hotter climates, investing in a higher SEER rating is more beneficial, while in milder climates, the additional cost may not yield significant savings.

Budget: Balancing upfront costs with long-term savings is essential. Higher SEER units generally cost more but offer greater efficiency and savings over time.

Tips for Saving Energy

Regular Maintenance:

Clean and Replace Filters: Dirty filters reduce airflow and efficiency. Regular cleaning or replacement ensures optimal performance.

Inspect and Seal Ducts: Leaky ducts can waste up to 20% of the energy used for heating and cooling. Regular inspections and sealing prevent this loss.

Optimize Thermostat Settings:

Programmable Thermostats: Use programmable or smart thermostats to adjust temperatures based on occupancy and time of day, reducing energy consumption when heating or cooling is unnecessary.

Seasonal Adjustments: Adjust thermostat settings seasonally. For instance, set the thermostat to a higher temperature in summer and a lower temperature in winter to save energy.

Upgrade Insulation:

Improve Insulation: Proper insulation in walls, ceilings, and floors helps maintain indoor temperatures and reduces the workload on HVAC systems.

Seal Gaps and Leaks: Use weatherstripping and caulking to seal gaps around doors, windows, and other openings to prevent energy loss.

HighEfficiency Equipment Choices

EnergyEfficient HVAC Systems:

Heat Pumps: Modern heat pumps are highly efficient for both heating and cooling, often with high SEER and HSPF (Heating Seasonal Performance Factor) ratings.

High-Efficiency Furnaces: Look for furnaces with an Annual Fuel Utilization Efficiency (AFUE) rating of 90% or higher for improved performance and reduced fuel consumption.

Advanced Technologies:

Variable Speed Compressors: These compressors adjust their speed to match the cooling load, providing better efficiency and comfort.

Zoning Systems: Zoning allows for targeted heating and cooling in different areas of a building, reducing energy waste by only conditioning occupied spaces.

Energy Audits

Purpose and Benefits:

Identify Energy Losses: An energy audit helps identify areas where energy is being wasted and provides recommendations for improvements.

Improve Efficiency: Recommendations from an audit can lead to more efficient HVAC operation and reduced energy costs.

Types of Energy Audits:

Professional Audits: Conducted by certified energy auditors, these audits use specialized tools to assess energy usage and provide a comprehensive report with improvement suggestions.

DIY Audits: Homeowners can perform basic audits by checking for visible signs of energy inefficiency, such as drafty windows or outdated insulation.

Renewable Energy Integration

Solar Energy:

Solar Panels: Installing solar panels can reduce reliance on grid electricity, lowering energy bills and the environmental impact of HVAC systems.

Solar Water Heating: Solar water heaters can supplement conventional water heating systems, providing hot water more efficiently.

Geothermal Systems:

Geothermal Heat Pumps: These systems use the earth's stable temperature to heat and cool buildings efficiently, offering significant energy savings and reducing operating costs.

EnergyEfficient Building Design

Building Envelope:

Insulation and Windows: Designing with high-quality insulation and energy-efficient windows reduces the need for excessive heating and cooling.

Reflective Roofing: Reflective or "cool" roofs can help lower cooling costs by reflecting more sunlight and absorbing less heat.

Design Principles:

Passive Solar Design: Utilize natural sunlight and building orientation to reduce the need for artificial heating and cooling.

Natural Ventilation: Design for natural airflow through windows, vents, and other openings to reduce the need for mechanical cooling.

Case Studies in Efficiency

Case Study 1: Office Building Retrofit

Project A large office building underwent a retrofit to improve energy efficiency, including upgrades to HVAC systems, insulation, and lighting.

Approach and Solutions: Replaced old HVAC units with highSEER models, improved insulation, and implemented a smart lighting system.

Results: Reduced energy consumption by 35% and achieved a return on investment within three years.

Case Study 2: Residential Solar Integration

Project A residential property integrated solar panels to supplement HVAC system energy needs.

Approach and Solutions: Installed a 5kW solar panel system and upgraded the HVAC system to a high-efficiency heat pump.

Results: Lowered monthly energy bills by 40% and reduced the household's carbon footprint by 25%.

Chapter 26: Insulation and Sealing

Types of Insulation

Fiberglass Insulation:

Description: Composed of tiny glass fibers, fiberglass insulation is a popular choice due to its affordability and effectiveness.

Forms: Available as batts, rolls, or loosefill. It's suitable for walls, attics, and floors.

Benefits: Provides good thermal resistance and soundproofing.

Foam Board Insulation:

Description: Rigid foam boards made from polystyrene, polyisocyanurate, or polyurethane.

Applications: Ideal for insulating foundations, walls, and roofs due to its high R-value per inch.

Benefits: Offers excellent thermal resistance and moisture resistance.

Spray Foam Insulation:

Description: Applied as a liquid that expands into a foam, filling gaps and crevices.

Types: Open-cell and closed-cell spray foams. Closed is denser and provides better insulation and moisture resistance.

Benefits: Provides an airtight seal, reducing air leaks and improving energy efficiency.

Reflective or Radiant Barrier Insulation:

Description: Made of reflective materials, such as aluminum foil, designed to reduce heat transfer.

Applications: Typically used in attics to reflect radiant heat away from living spaces.

Benefits: Effective in hot climates where cooling is a priority.

Techniques for Air Sealing

Identifying Air Leaks:

Visual Inspection: Check for gaps around windows, doors, and other openings.

Smoke Test: Use smoke pencils or incense sticks to identify drafts and leaks.

Sealing Methods:

Weatherstripping: Apply weatherstripping around the doors and windows to seal gaps and improve insulation.

Caulking: Use caulk to fill gaps and cracks in walls, around windows, and near baseboards.

Foam Sealant: Apply expanding foam sealant to larger gaps around plumbing, electrical outlets, and in attics or crawl spaces.

Common Areas to Seal:

Windows and Doors: Seal around frames and between sashes to prevent drafts.

Attics and Basements: Seal gaps in attic hatches, basement windows, and around ductwork.

Insulation Installation Procedures
Preparation:
Assess Existing Conditions: Check the condition of existing insulation and address any moisture or damage issues.
Choose Insulation Type: Select the appropriate type of insulation based on the area and climate.
Installation Steps:
Fiberglass Batts: Cut to fit between studs or joists. Ensure a snug fit without compressing the material.
Foam Board: Cut panels to size and fit them between wall studs or under floors. Seal edges with tape or foam sealant.
Spray Foam: Apply foam in layers, allowing each layer to cure before applying the next. Ensure complete coverage of gaps and crevices.
Safety Considerations:
Protective Gear: Wear gloves, masks, and protective eyewear when handling insulation materials.
Ventilation: Ensure proper ventilation when using spray foam or working in enclosed spaces.

Assessing Existing Insulation
Inspection Techniques:
Visual Inspection: Check for signs of damage, such as sagging, compression, or mold growth.
Thermal Imaging: Use thermal cameras to identify areas with insufficient insulation or air leaks.
Evaluating Effectiveness:
RValue: Determine the R-value of existing insulation to assess its effectiveness. Compare with current standards and recommendations.
Energy Bills: Analyze changes in energy bills to identify potential areas where insulation may be insufficient.
Upgrading Insulation:
Determine Needs: Based on the assessment, decide if additional insulation is needed or if replacement is necessary.
Choose Appropriate Insulation: Select insulation materials and methods that will improve the current thermal resistance and energy efficiency.

Impact on Energy Efficiency
Benefits of Proper Insulation:
Reduced Energy Consumption: Wellinsulated homes require less heating and cooling, leading to lower energy bills.
Improved Comfort: Proper insulation maintains consistent indoor temperatures, enhancing comfort.
Extended HVAC Life: Reduced workload on HVAC systems can extend their lifespan and reduce maintenance needs.

Energy Savings Potential:

Quantifying Savings: Energy audits can estimate potential savings from improved insulation and sealing.

Cost vs. Benefit: Compare the cost of insulation upgrades with the long-term energy savings and benefits.

Thermal Imaging for Inspections

Purpose of Thermal Imaging:

Detecting Heat Loss: Thermal imaging cameras can visualize temperature differences and identify areas of heat loss or insufficient insulation.

Identifying Air Leaks: Helps pinpoint gaps and leaks that are not visible through regular inspections.

How Thermal Imaging Works:

Infrared Technology: Cameras detect infrared radiation emitted by objects and convert it into a visible image.

Analysis: Analyze thermal images to locate temperature anomalies and assess insulation effectiveness.

Limitations:

Cost: Thermal imaging equipment can be expensive, but it provides valuable insights for large-scale or complex inspections.

Training Required: Proper interpretation of thermal images requires training and experience.

Case Studies in Insulation

Case Study 1: Residential Insulation Upgrade

Project A homeowner upgraded insulation in an older house to improve energy efficiency.

Approach: Replaced fiberglass batts with spray foam insulation in walls and attic. Added additional fiberglass batts in the basement.

Results: Reduced heating costs by 30% and improved overall comfort. The payback period for the investment was estimated at five years.

Case Study 2: Commercial Building Retrofit

Project A commercial building underwent an insulation retrofit to reduce energy consumption and meet new building codes.

Approach: Installed high-performance foam board insulation on exterior walls and upgraded attic insulation. Sealed air leaks throughout the building.

Results: Achieved a 25% reduction in energy costs and improved indoor air quality. Enhanced building performance led to higher tenant satisfaction.

Book 7:

Advanced HVAC Systems and Technologies

Chapter 27: Variable Refrigerant Flow (VRF) Systems

Basics and Applications
What is VRF?
Definition: Variable Refrigerant Flow (VRF) systems are advanced HVAC systems that use refrigerant as the cooling and heating medium. They provide flexibility in temperature control and energy efficiency by adjusting the refrigerant flow based on the load requirements of different zones.

Functionality: VRF systems use a single outdoor unit connected to multiple indoor units. The system modulates the amount of refrigerant sent to each indoor unit, allowing for precise temperature control in individual zones.

Applications:
Commercial Buildings: Ideal for office buildings, hotels, and retail spaces where multiple zones require independent temperature control.

Residential Buildings: Suitable for large homes or multifamily buildings seeking efficient and customizable climate control.

Mixed-Use Buildings: Effective in structures combining residential and commercial spaces, allowing for varied temperature settings in different areas.

Installation and Maintenance Practices
Installation:
Site Assessment: Evaluate the building layout, load requirements, and available space for both indoor and outdoor units.

Component Placement: Install outdoor units in accessible locations for maintenance. Position indoor units strategically to ensure even air distribution.

Piping and Wiring: Properly size and install refrigerant piping and electrical wiring. Follow manufacturer guidelines to ensure system performance and reliability.

Commissioning: After installation, perform system checks to verify proper operation, refrigerant levels, and connectivity between components.

Maintenance:
Regular Inspections: Conduct routine inspections to check for leaks, component wear, and overall system performance.

Cleaning: Clean filters, coils, and condensate drains regularly to maintain efficiency and prevent issues.

Refrigerant Checks: Monitor refrigerant levels and pressures to ensure optimal performance and address any leaks promptly.

System Upgrades: Stay updated with the latest VRF technology advancements and consider upgrades for improved efficiency and functionality.

Advantages and Disadvantages
Advantages:

Energy Efficiency: VRF systems adjust refrigerant flow to match the cooling or heating demand, leading to significant energy savings compared to traditional systems.

Flexible Zoning: Individual control of multiple zones allows for personalized comfort and reduced energy waste in unoccupied areas.

Quiet Operation: Indoor units are designed to operate quietly, enhancing the comfort level within the space.

SpaceSaving Design: Compact indoor units and a single outdoor unit save space and provide aesthetic benefits.

Disadvantages:

High Initial Cost: The initial cost of VRF systems can be higher than traditional HVAC systems, which may be a consideration for some projects.

Complex Installation: Installation requires specialized knowledge and skills, making it essential to work with experienced professionals.

Maintenance Costs: Although generally low, maintenance costs can be higher due to the complexity of the system and the need for specialized technicians.

VRF System Components

Outdoor Unit:

Function: Houses the compressor and condensing coil. It handles the heat exchange with the outdoor air.

Features: Includes variable-speed compressors and advanced controls to manage refrigerant flow.

Indoor Units:

Types: Wall-mounted, ceiling-mounted, cassette, and ducted units, each designed for specific installation and aesthetic needs.

Function: Distributes conditioned air throughout the space and allows for individual temperature control in different zones.

Refrigerant Piping:

Description: The network of pipes that carry refrigerant between the outdoor and indoor units.

Insulation: Proper insulation is essential to prevent energy loss and ensure efficient operation.

Controls:

Thermostats and Controllers: Manage the operation of the indoor units and adjust settings for each zone.

Building Management Systems (BMS): Integrate VRF systems with broader building control systems for enhanced management and monitoring.

VRF System Configurations

Single Split Configuration:

Description: One outdoor unit is connected to one indoor unit. Suitable for small applications where individual zone control is not required.

Applications: Single-room offices or small residential units.

Multi Split Configuration:

Description: One outdoor unit connected to multiple indoor units. Allows for zoning and customized temperature control in various spaces.

Applications: Commercial spaces with multiple rooms or offices.

Heat Recovery Configuration:

Description: Allows simultaneous heating and cooling in different zones by recovering waste heat from one area to use in another.

Applications: Buildings with varying heating and cooling needs, such as mixed-use buildings or hotels.

Heat Pump Configuration:

Description: Provides either heating or cooling, but not simultaneously. Offers efficient temperature control for spaces with uniform needs.

Applications: Buildings with similar heating and cooling demands throughout the year.

Energy Efficiency of VRF Systems

SEER and EER Ratings:

SEER (Seasonal Energy Efficiency Ratio): Measures cooling efficiency over an entire season. Higher SEER ratings indicate better efficiency.

EER (Energy Efficiency Ratio): Measures cooling efficiency at a specific operating condition. Higher EER ratings reflect better performance.

Energy Savings Potential:

Demand-based Operation: VRF systems adjust refrigerant flow based on real-time load requirements, leading to reduced energy consumption.

Zoning Benefits: Individual zone control reduces energy use in unoccupied areas, contributing to overall savings.

Impact on Building Performance:

Reduced Operational Costs: Lower energy consumption translates to reduced utility bills and operational costs.

Enhanced Comfort: Precise temperature control improves occupant comfort and satisfaction.

Case Studies in VRF Implementation

Case Study 1: Office Building Retrofit

Project An office building with outdated HVAC systems upgraded to a VRF system to enhance energy efficiency and comfort.

Implementation: Replaced old rooftop units with a VRF system featuring multiple indoor units for individual office control.

Results: Achieved a 35% reduction in energy consumption and improved employee comfort. The payback period is estimated at four years.

Case Study 2: Hotel HVAC Upgrade

Project A hotel with diverse climate control needs in different guest rooms and common areas installed a VRF system for efficient management.

Implementation: Installed a heat recovery VRF system to provide simultaneous heating and cooling across various zones.

Results: Reduced energy costs by 40% and increased guest satisfaction due to better climate control. Improved system flexibility supported the hotel's diverse needs.

Chapter 28: Geothermal Heat Pumps

Principles and Benefits

What is a Geothermal Heat Pump?

Definition: A geothermal heat pump (GHP) is an HVAC system that utilizes the Earth's stable underground temperature to provide heating, cooling, and hot water. It extracts or rejects heat from/to the ground or a water source, leveraging the Earth's natural thermal energy.

Principle of Operation: The system uses a ground loop to transfer heat between the building and the ground. During winter, it extracts heat from the ground to warm the building. In summer, it reverses the process, transferring heat from the building back into the ground.

Benefits:

Energy Efficiency: Geothermal heat pumps are highly efficient because they use the Earth's relatively constant temperature, leading to lower energy consumption compared to conventional HVAC systems.

Environmental Impact: They have a minimal environmental footprint since they reduce reliance on fossil fuels and lower greenhouse gas emissions.

Longevity: GHP systems have a long lifespan, often exceeding 25 years for the indoor components and up to 50 years for the ground loop.

Comfort: Provides consistent and even heating and cooling, maintaining a stable indoor climate year-round.

Steps for Installation

Site Assessment:

Geological Survey: Conduct a geological survey to assess soil conditions, groundwater levels, and thermal properties. This ensures suitable ground conditions for the heat pump installation.

System Sizing: Determine the appropriate size of the geothermal system based on the building's heating and cooling load requirements.

Ground Loop Installation:

Vertical Loops: Boreholes are drilled vertically into the ground, and heat exchange pipes are inserted. Suitable for properties with limited space.

Horizontal Loops: Pipes are laid out horizontally in trenches, ideal for larger areas with sufficient land. Typically less expensive than vertical loops.

Pond/Lake Loops: Used if a nearby water source is available. Pipes are submerged in the water to exchange heat. This option requires careful consideration of environmental impact.

Indoor Unit Installation:

Heat Pump Unit: Install the geothermal heat pump indoors, connecting it to the ground loop and the building's ductwork or hydronic system.

Distribution System: Integrate with existing or new ductwork (for air systems) or piping (for hydronic systems) to distribute conditioned air or water throughout the building.

System Testing and Commissioning:

System Checks: Verify all connections, refrigerant levels, and operational settings. Ensure that the system operates efficiently and effectively.

Performance Testing: Run the system to confirm that it meets performance expectations and heating/cooling loads.

Real World Case Studies

Case Study 1: Residential Application

Project A residential home in a rural area installed a geothermal heat pump system to replace an aging oil furnace.

Implementation: Installed vertical ground loops due to limited yard space and integrated with existing ductwork.

Results: Achieved a 50% reduction in energy bills and significant improvement in indoor comfort. The system paid for itself in approximately seven years.

Case Study 2: Commercial Building Retrofit

Project A commercial office building in an urban setting upgraded to a geothermal heat pump system to improve energy efficiency and reduce operational costs.

Implementation: Implemented horizontal ground loops due to available space and integrated with a new ductless distribution system.

Results: Reduced annual energy costs by 40% and improved tenant satisfaction due to enhanced climate control. The system's ROI was realized within five years.

Ground Loop Designs

Vertical Ground Loops:

Design Considerations: The depth and spacing of boreholes are crucial for efficient heat exchange. Boreholes typically range from 100 to 400 feet deep.

Installation: Requires specialized drilling equipment and should be conducted by experienced professionals to ensure proper placement and performance.

Horizontal Ground Loops:

Design Considerations: Trench depth and width are critical for maintaining heat exchange efficiency. Typically installed 4 to 6 feet deep in trenches.

Installation: Involves excavation and pipe placement in trenches, followed by backfilling. Less intrusive than vertical loops but requires sufficient land area.

Pond/Lake Loops:

Design Considerations: Requires an assessment of water quality and environmental impact. Loop placement should avoid disrupting aquatic life.

Installation: Involves submerging pipes in a pond or lake and connecting them to the heat pump system. Ideal for properties with access to clean, stable water sources.

Efficiency Considerations
Coefficient of Performance (COP):
Definition: A measure of a heat pump's efficiency, calculated as the ratio of heat output to electrical energy input. Higher COP values indicate better efficiency.
Typical Values: Geothermal heat pumps generally have COPs ranging from 0 to 0, significantly higher than traditional systems.
Seasonal Performance:
Heating Season Efficiency: GHPs maintain high efficiency during cold weather due to the stable ground temperature.
Cooling Season Efficiency: The system's efficiency remains high in hot weather, as the ground acts as a heat sink.
System Sizing and Load Matching:
Proper Sizing: Accurate load calculations are essential to ensure the system meets heating and cooling demands efficiently without overworking.

Maintenance Requirements
Routine Maintenance:
Filter Replacement: Regularly replace or clean air filters to maintain system efficiency and air quality.
Loop Inspections: Periodically inspect the ground loop for leaks or damage, especially if there are signs of system performance issues.
System Checks:
Heat Pump Inspection: Have the heat pump unit inspected by a professional annually to check refrigerant levels, connections, and overall performance.
Pump and Fan Maintenance: Ensure that the circulating pump and fans are functioning correctly and lubricated as needed.
Troubleshooting:
Performance Issues: Address any issues related to reduced performance, unusual noises, or system malfunctions promptly to avoid costly repairs.

Cost and ROI Analysis
Initial Costs:
Installation Costs: Geothermal heat pumps generally have higher upfront costs compared to conventional systems, including the installation of ground loops and indoor units.
Operational Savings:
Energy Costs: Significant savings on energy bills due to high efficiency and reduced reliance on fossil fuels.

Maintenance Costs: Lower maintenance costs compared to traditional systems due to fewer moving parts and reduced wear and tear.

Return on Investment (ROI):

Payback Period: Typically ranges from 5 to 10 years, depending on energy savings, installation costs, and local energy prices.

Long-Term Benefits: Considerable long-term savings and environmental benefits make geothermal heat pumps a cost-effective choice over their lifespan.

Chapter 29: Hydronic Heating Systems

Radiant Floor Heating Systems

Definition: Radiant floor heating systems use warm water circulating through pipes or cables embedded in the floor to provide consistent and comfortable heat. It can be installed in new construction or retrofitted into existing buildings.

Types:

Warm Water Systems: Utilize a network of PEX (crosslinked polyethylene) tubing embedded in the floor, heated by a boiler.

Electric Systems: Use electric cables or mats installed beneath the flooring. Generally used for smaller areas or as supplementary heat.

Advantages:

Comfort: Provides even heat distribution, reducing cold spots and eliminating the need for radiators or baseboards.

Energy Efficiency: Lower operating costs due to reduced need for high-temperature water; operates effectively with lower temperatures.

Aesthetics: No visible heating elements or bulky radiators, allowing for flexible interior design.

Disadvantages:

Installation Cost: Higher initial installation cost compared to traditional heating methods.

Flooring Types: Some flooring materials, such as hardwood, may require specific considerations or treatments.

Baseboard Heating Solutions

Definition: Baseboard heaters are a type of hydronic or electric heating system that provides heat through units installed along the baseboards of a room.

Types:

Hydronic Baseboard Heaters: Use hot water from a boiler, circulating through pipes in baseboard units.

Electric Baseboard Heaters: Use electrical resistance to generate heat.

Advantages:

Easy Installation: Typically simpler and less expensive to install compared to radiant floor heating systems.

Zoning: Allows for individual room temperature control, enhancing comfort and energy efficiency.

Disadvantages:

Space Usage: Units are visible and occupy wall space, which can affect furniture placement.

Heating Efficiency: Generally less efficient than radiant systems for whole-house heating.

Hydronic Boiler Options

Types of Boilers:

Conventional Boilers: Traditional units that heat water to high temperatures and circulate it through the system. Suitable for use with radiators and baseboard heaters.

Condensing Boilers: High-efficiency boilers that extract additional heat from exhaust gases, improving overall system efficiency. Ideal for hydronic systems with low return temperatures.

Combination Boilers (Combi Boilers): Provide both space heating and domestic hot water in one unit, suitable for smaller homes or apartments.

Selection Criteria:

Size and Capacity: Choose a boiler with the appropriate capacity for the heating load of the building.

Fuel Type: Options include natural gas, oil, propane, and electric. Select based on availability and cost of fuel.

Efficiency Ratings: Consider efficiency ratings such as Annual Fuel Utilization Efficiency (AFUE) to ensure cost-effective operation.

System Components and Layouts

Key Components:

Boiler: The central heating unit that heats the water.

Piping: Pipes distribute hot water throughout the system. Common materials include PEX, copper, and steel.

Radiators/Baseboards: Heat emitters that transfer heat from the hot water to the room.

Expansion Tank: Compensates for changes in water volume due to temperature fluctuations.

Circulator Pump: Ensures continuous water flow through the system.

Layouts:

ClosedLoop System: Water circulates in a sealed loop, with no need for replenishing water. Commonly used in residential settings.

OpenLoop System: Water is drawn from a source (e.g., well) and discharged after use. Less common in residential applications due to potential water quality issues.

Installation and Maintenance

Installation Steps:

System Design: Plan the layout, including boiler placement, pipe routing, and heat emitter locations. Perform a load calculation to ensure proper sizing.

Piping Installation: Lay out and connect the piping according to the system design. Ensure proper insulation to minimize heat loss.

Boiler Installation: Install the boiler, connecting it to the piping system and any necessary controls.

Testing: Fill the system with water, check for leaks, and ensure all components are functioning correctly.

Maintenance Tips:
Regular Inspections: Check for leaks, air in the system, and proper operation of the circulator pump.
Annual Service: Have the boiler serviced annually by a professional to ensure optimal performance and efficiency.
Bleeding Radiators/Baseboards: Remove air from the system periodically to maintain efficient heat transfer.

Efficiency and Performance
Efficiency Considerations:
Boiler Efficiency: Higher-efficiency boilers reduce fuel consumption and operating costs. Look for units with high AFUE ratings.
System Design: Proper design and installation are critical for achieving optimal efficiency. Ensure that the system is sized correctly and components are properly installed.
Performance Factors:
Heat Distribution: Ensure even heat distribution throughout the building to avoid cold spots and maintain comfort.
System Balancing: Adjust flow rates and temperatures to balance the system and optimize performance.

Case Studies in Hydronic Heating
Case Study 1: Residential Application
Project A homeowner in a cold climate installed a hydronic heating system to replace an outdated electric baseboard system.
Implementation: Installed radiant floor heating in the main living areas and baseboard heaters in secondary rooms. Choose a high-efficiency condensing boiler.
Results: Reduced heating costs by 40% and improved overall comfort. The system's flexibility allowed for customized heating in different zones.
Case Study 2: Commercial Building
Project A commercial building retrofit included the installation of a hydronic heating system to improve energy efficiency and comfort.
Implementation: Used a combination of radiant floor heating and baseboard heaters with a new high-efficiency boiler. Designed the system for optimal heat distribution in the building.
Results: Achieved a 35% reduction in energy costs and enhanced comfort for occupants. The system's design allowed for effective temperature control in different areas of the building.

Chapter 30: Smart HVAC Solutions

Smart Thermostat Technologies

Definition: Smart thermostats are advanced temperature control devices that can be programmed and controlled remotely via a smartphone, tablet, or computer. They use sensors, algorithms, and connectivity to optimize HVAC system performance and energy use.

Key Features:

Learning Capabilities: Some smart thermostats learn from user behavior and automatically adjust settings to improve comfort and efficiency.

Geofencing: Detects when users are away from home and adjusts settings accordingly to save energy.

Voice Control: Many models integrate with voice assistants like Amazon Alexa or Google Assistant for hands-free operation.

Installation and Setup:

Compatibility Check: Ensure the thermostat is compatible with the existing HVAC system.

Wiring and Mounting: Follow manufacturer instructions for wiring and mounting the thermostat.

Configuration: Set up WiFi connectivity and configure preferences via the mobile app or web interface.

Integrating Home Automation

Definition: Home automation involves the use of technology to control various aspects of a home's systems, including HVAC, lighting, security, and more, from a central interface or remotely.

Integration with HVAC: Smart HVAC systems can be seamlessly integrated with home automation platforms to enhance comfort, convenience, and energy efficiency.

Common Automation Features:

Scheduling: Program HVAC systems to adjust temperatures based on daily routines or special events.

Scenes and Routines: Create scenes that adjust multiple devices simultaneously, such as the "Away" mode that lowers the temperature when everyone leaves the house.

IoT Applications in HVAC

Definition: The Internet of Things (IoT) refers to the network of interconnected devices that communicate and share data over the internet. In HVAC, IoT applications enhance system monitoring, control, and maintenance.

Benefits:

RealTime Monitoring: Track HVAC system performance and environmental conditions in real-time.

Predictive Maintenance: Use data analytics to predict and prevent potential system failures before they occur.

IoT Components:

Sensors: Monitor temperature, humidity, and air quality. Data from these sensors helps in adjusting system settings for optimal performance.

Controllers: Devices that receive data from sensors and adjust HVAC settings accordingly. Can be integrated with cloud-based platforms for remote access.

Remote Monitoring and Control

Definition: Remote monitoring and control allow users to manage their HVAC systems from anywhere using mobile apps, web interfaces, or voice commands.

Features:

Temperature Adjustments: Change temperature settings remotely to ensure comfort before arriving home.

System Alerts: Receive notifications about system issues or maintenance needs directly on mobile devices.

Benefits:

Convenience: Control HVAC systems from anywhere, whether at home or away.

Energy Savings: Adjust settings based on real-time conditions and occupancy to save energy.

Applications:

Mobile Apps: Apps from HVAC manufacturers or third-party platforms provide user-friendly interfaces for remote management.

Web Portals: Access system data and control settings through web-based portals for more detailed management.

Energy Management Systems

Definition: Energy management systems (EMS) optimize energy use in buildings by monitoring and controlling HVAC systems, lighting, and other energy-consuming devices.

Components:

Sensors and Meters: Track energy consumption and identify areas for improvement.

Control Systems: Automate adjustments to HVAC settings based on real-time data and predefined rules.

Benefits:

Cost Savings: Reduce energy bills by optimizing system performance and identifying inefficiencies.

Sustainability: Lower carbon footprint by improving energy efficiency and integrating renewable energy sources.

Implementation:

System Design: Develop a tailored EMS solution based on the building's energy needs and goals.

Data Analysis: Use data collected from sensors and meters to make informed decisions about energy use and conservation.

Smart Building Solutions

Definition: Smart building solutions integrate various technologies to enhance the functionality, efficiency, and comfort of buildings. HVAC is a critical component of these systems.

Features:

Building Automation Systems (BAS): Centralized systems that control HVAC, lighting, security, and other building functions.

Integration with IoT: Connects HVAC systems with other building systems to optimize performance and energy use.

Benefits:

Enhanced Comfort: Automatically adjusts environmental conditions to meet occupants' needs.

Operational Efficiency: Streamlines building management and reduces operational costs.

Case Studies:

Office Buildings: Implemented smart HVAC systems to improve energy efficiency and occupant comfort. Results included reduced energy consumption and enhanced productivity.

Retail Spaces: Used smart HVAC solutions to create optimal shopping environments while managing energy costs effectively.

Future Trends in Smart HVAC

Emerging Technologies: The HVAC industry is continuously evolving with advancements in technology, leading to more sophisticated and efficient systems.

Trends to Watch:

Increased Integration with AI: AI-driven HVAC systems will offer even more precise control and predictive maintenance capabilities.

Enhanced User Interfaces: Future systems will feature more intuitive and user-friendly interfaces, including advanced voice and gesture controls.

Greater Focus on Sustainability: Increased emphasis on energy-efficient technologies and integration with renewable energy sources.

Impact on the Industry:

Improved Efficiency: Ongoing advancements will lead to even more energy-efficient systems and reduced environmental impact.

Greater Convenience: Innovations will make it easier for users to manage their HVAC systems and integrate them with other smart home technologies.

Chapter 31: Ductless HVAC Systems

Mini Split Systems Explained

Definition: Mini-split systems are a type of ductless HVAC system that provides heating and cooling to individual rooms or zones without the need for ductwork. They consist of an indoor unit and an outdoor unit connected by refrigerant lines.

Components:
Indoor Unit: Mounted on a wall or ceiling, it blows conditioned air directly into the room.
Outdoor Unit: Houses the compressor and condenser, which are responsible for transferring heat.
Refrigerant Lines: Carry refrigerant between the indoor and outdoor units.

Operation:
Cooling Mode: The indoor unit absorbs heat from the room and transfers it to the outdoor unit, which releases it.
Heating Mode: The process is reversed, with the system extracting heat from the outside air and transferring it indoors.

Multi Split System Applications

Definition: Multi-split systems are an extension of mini-split systems, allowing multiple indoor units to be connected to a single outdoor unit. This setup provides flexibility in controlling the temperature of different zones or rooms.

Configuration:
Indoor Units: These can include various types such as wall-mounted, ceiling cassette, or floor-mounted units.
Outdoor Unit: Manages the operation of multiple indoor units, offering centralized control.

Applications:
Residential: Ideal for homes with multiple rooms or zones requiring individual temperature control.
Commercial: Suitable for office spaces, retail stores, and other businesses that need to manage temperature in different areas.

Benefits and Use Cases

Benefits:
Energy Efficiency: Mini-split systems are highly efficient because they avoid the energy losses associated with ductwork. They provide targeted heating and cooling, reducing energy consumption.
Zoned Comfort: Allows for different temperatures in different rooms or zones, improving comfort and satisfaction.
Flexibility: Easy to install and configure, making them suitable for both new constructions and retrofits.

Use Cases:
Retrofits: Ideal for homes or buildings where installing ductwork is impractical or costly.

Additions and Renovations: Perfect for adding climate control to new rooms or extensions without extending existing ductwork.

Installation and Maintenance

Installation:
Site Assessment: Evaluate the space to determine the best locations for indoor and outdoor units.
Mounting Indoor Units: Install indoor units on walls, ceilings, or floors as required, ensuring proper clearance for airflow.
Outdoor Unit Placement: Position the outdoor unit on a stable surface, such as a concrete pad or mounting bracket.
Refrigerant Lines: Connect refrigerant lines and electrical wiring between indoor and outdoor units.

Maintenance:
Regular Cleaning: Clean filters, coils, and drain lines to maintain system performance and efficiency.
Seasonal Checkups: Inspect refrigerant levels, electrical connections, and overall system operation at least once a year.
Professional Service: Schedule annual maintenance with a certified technician to ensure optimal performance and longevity.

Energy Efficiency

Efficiency Ratings:
SEER (Seasonal Energy Efficiency Ratio): Measures cooling efficiency. Higher SEER ratings indicate better efficiency.
HSPF (Heating Seasonal Performance Factor): Measures heating efficiency. Higher HSPF ratings represent better performance.

Improvement Tips:
Insulation: Ensure proper insulation in the rooms served by the mini-split system to reduce energy loss.
Temperature Settings: Set thermostats to moderate temperatures and avoid extreme settings to enhance efficiency.
Regular Maintenance: Perform regular maintenance to keep the system running efficiently and prevent energy waste.

Case Studies in Ductless HVAC

Case Study 1: Residential Retrofit
Scenario: The homeowner needed an efficient cooling solution for a house without existing ductwork.
Solution: Installed a mini-split system with three indoor units connected to a single outdoor unit.
Outcome: Enhanced comfort with individualized temperature control and reduced energy costs.

Case Study 2: Commercial Office Space
Scenario: Office building required climate control for different zones due to varied occupancy and use.
Solution: Implemented a multi-split system with multiple indoor units servicing different office areas.

Outcome: Improved comfort and energy efficiency, with the ability to adjust temperatures based on room usage.

Case Study 3: Home Addition

Scenario: New room addition needed climate control without extending existing ductwork.

Solution: Installed a mini-split system to provide heating and cooling for the new space.

Outcome: Seamless integration with the existing home, providing efficient climate control without disrupting existing systems.

Book 8:

HVAC Regulations, Standards, and Business Guide

Chapter 32: Understanding Building Codes

Local and National Code Requirements

Building Codes: Regulations set by local, state, and national authorities to ensure safety, health, and efficiency in building construction and HVAC system installations.

Local Codes: Specific to a municipality or county, these codes address regional needs and conditions, such as climate and local building practices.

National Codes: Established by organizations like the International Code Council (ICC) and the American Society of Heating, Refrigerating, and AirConditioning Engineers (ASHRAE), providing a uniform standard across the country.

Key Organizations:

International Code Council (ICC): Develops the International Building Code (IBC) and other codes related to HVAC systems.

American Society of Heating, Refrigerating, and AirConditioning Engineers (ASHRAE): Publishes standards like ASHRAE 61 for ventilation and ASHRAE 90.1 for energy efficiency.

National Fire Protection Association (NFPA): Sets standards for fire safety, including those relevant to HVAC systems.

Ensuring Compliance

Importance of Compliance:

Safety: Ensures that HVAC systems are installed and operated safely, minimizing risks such as fires, gas leaks, and electrical hazards.

Efficiency: Helps in achieving energy efficiency and reducing operational costs, as codes often include requirements for energy-saving measures.

Legal Requirements: Compliance with building codes is mandatory and helps avoid legal issues and fines.

Steps for Ensuring Compliance:

Research Codes: Familiarize yourself with the relevant codes for your area and specific project requirements.

Design Adherence: Ensure that HVAC system designs meet code requirements from the outset.

Documentation: Maintain accurate records of compliance measures, including design plans, permits, and inspection reports.

Consult Professionals: Work with code experts, engineers, or inspectors to ensure all aspects of the installation meet code requirements.

Updates and Amendments to Codes

Keeping up to date:

Code Revision Cycles: Building codes are periodically updated to incorporate new technologies, address emerging issues, and improve safety and efficiency.

Review Processes: Follow the processes for code updates and amendments, which may include public comments, committee reviews, and formal adoption.

Impact of Updates:

Design Changes: New or amended codes may require modifications to existing designs or installation practices.

Training: Stay informed about changes to ensure that all team members are aware of and understand new requirements.

Sources for Updates:

Code Authorities: Regularly check with local code enforcement agencies and national code organizations for updates.

Professional Associations: Join industry associations and participate in training or continuing education opportunities to stay informed.

Code Compliance Inspections

Inspection Process:

Scheduling Inspections: Plan inspections according to project milestones, such as after installation or before system startup.

Inspection Criteria: Understand what inspectors will be looking for, including adherence to code requirements, proper installation practices, and documentation.

Common Findings: Be prepared to address common issues such as inadequate clearances, incorrect duct sizes, or improper refrigerant handling.

Preparing for Inspections:

PreInspection Check: Conduct internal reviews to identify and correct potential issues before the official inspection.

Documentation: Ensure all required permits, plans, and compliance records are readily available for the inspector.

Common Code Violations

Examples of Violations:

Improper Ventilation: Failure to provide adequate ventilation or incorrect installation of ventilation systems.

Electrical Issues: Noncompliance with electrical codes, such as incorrect wiring or insufficient grounding.

Inadequate Clearances: Failure to maintain required clearances around HVAC equipment, can affect safety and maintenance.

Avoiding Violations:

Adherence to Codes: Follow all code requirements carefully during design and installation.

Regular Reviews: Conduct regular reviews of code requirements and best practices to ensure compliance.

Impact on System Design

Design Considerations:

Efficiency Standards: Incorporate energy efficiency requirements into system design, such as minimum SEER ratings and insulation levels.

Safety Features: Design systems with safety features that meet or exceed code requirements, such as proper ventilation and fire safety measures.

Accessibility: Ensure that systems are designed for easy maintenance and compliance with accessibility requirements.

Integration with Building Design:

Holistic Approach: Work with architects and engineers to integrate HVAC design with overall building design and code requirements.

Adaptation: Be prepared to adapt designs based on site-specific conditions and code requirements.

Case Studies in Code Compliance

Case Study 1: Residential HVAC Installation

Scenario: Installation of a new HVAC system in a residential building required adherence to updated energy efficiency codes.

Solution: Conducted a thorough review of the latest codes and integrated required energy-saving measures into the system design.

Outcome: Successfully passed inspection and achieved significant energy savings for the homeowner.

Case Study 2: Commercial Building Retrofit

Scenario: Retrofitting an old commercial building with new HVAC systems while complying with current safety and efficiency codes.

Solution: Worked with code experts to address challenges related to outdated infrastructure and updated codes.

Outcome: Completed the retrofit with full code compliance and improved building performance.

Case Study 3: New Construction Project

Scenario: Designing and installing HVAC systems for a new commercial building with complex code requirements.

Solution: Collaborated with architects and engineers to ensure that all aspects of the HVAC design met code requirements from the beginning.
Outcome: Achieved successful code compliance and streamlined the inspection process.

Chapter 33: Safety Standards in HVAC

OSHA Guidelines

Occupational Safety and Health Administration (OSHA): A federal agency responsible for ensuring safe and healthy working conditions. OSHA sets standards and enforces regulations to prevent workplace injuries and illnesses.

Relevant Standards: OSHA has specific regulations for the HVAC industry, including guidelines on electrical safety, handling refrigerants, and working at heights.

Key Guidelines:

General Duty Clause: Employers must provide a workplace free from recognized hazards that are likely to cause death or serious physical harm.

Hazard Communication: Ensure proper labeling, training, and safety data sheets (SDS) for hazardous materials used in HVAC work.

Personal Protective Equipment (PPE): Requirements for PPE to protect against electrical hazards, chemical exposures, and physical injuries.

Implementation:

Compliance: Regularly review OSHA regulations and ensure that all practices and equipment meet the required standards.

Documentation: Maintain records of safety training, equipment inspections, and incident reports to demonstrate compliance.

Best Practices in the Industry

Safety Culture:

Promote Safety: Foster a culture where safety is a priority, encouraging employees to adhere to best practices and report potential hazards.

Leadership: Ensure that safety is a core value of leadership and is reflected in all organizational practices and policies.

Best Practices:

Use of PPE: Always wear appropriate PPE, such as gloves, safety glasses, and hearing protection, depending on the task.

Tool Safety: Regularly inspect and maintain tools and equipment to ensure they are in safe working condition.

Safe Work Procedures: Follow established procedures for handling refrigerants, and electrical components, and working in confined spaces.

Continuous Improvement:

Feedback Mechanism: Implement a system for employees to provide feedback on safety practices and suggest improvements.

Regular Reviews: Continuously review and update safety procedures based on industry developments and incident reports.

Electrical Safety Standards

National Electrical Code (NEC): Sets standards for electrical installations to ensure safety and reduce the risk of electrical hazards.

Key Areas: Electrical wiring, grounding, and circuit protection are critical components of electrical safety in HVAC systems.

Important Standards:

Wiring Methods: Follow NEC guidelines for wiring installations, including proper insulation and conduit use.

Grounding and Bonding: Ensure all electrical systems are properly grounded and bonded to prevent electrical shock and equipment damage.

Circuit Protection: Use circuit breakers and fuses to protect against overloads and short circuits.

Best Practices:

Qualified Personnel: Only trained and qualified personnel should perform electrical work on HVAC systems.

Regular Inspections: Conduct regular inspections and maintenance of electrical systems to identify and address potential hazards.

Safety Audits and Inspections

Purpose:

Identify Hazards: Safety audits and inspections help identify potential hazards and ensure compliance with safety regulations.

Verify Compliance: Regular audits ensure that safety procedures are being followed and that equipment is in good condition.

Process:

Scheduled Audits: Perform routine safety audits as part of your regular maintenance schedule.

Inspection Checklists: Use checklists to ensure that all aspects of safety are covered during inspections, including PPE use, equipment condition, and compliance with regulations.

FollowUp:

Corrective Actions: Address any issues identified during audits promptly, implementing corrective actions to prevent future occurrences.

Documentation: Keep detailed records of audits, inspections, and corrective actions taken.

Incident Reporting

Importance:

Record Keeping: Accurate incident reporting helps track safety performance and identify areas for improvement.

Legal Compliance: Reporting incidents following OSHA requirements ensures legal compliance and protects your business from potential liabilities.

Process:

Immediate Reporting: Report any incidents or near misses as soon as they occur to ensure prompt investigation and response.

Investigation: Conduct thorough investigations to determine the cause of the incident and prevent recurrence.

Documentation: Maintain detailed records of incidents, including causes, actions taken, and outcomes.

Safety Training Programs

Training Importance: Ongoing safety training ensures that employees are aware of safety practices and regulations and are prepared to handle potential hazards.

Types of Training: Includes general safety training, equipment-specific training, and emergency response training.

Program Components:

Orientation: Provide safety training as part of employee onboarding to ensure new hires are aware of safety procedures and regulations.

Ongoing Education: Offer regular refresher courses and updates on new safety standards and practices.

Practical Training: Include hands-on training to familiarize employees with the safe use of tools and equipment.

Evaluation:

Training Effectiveness: Regularly evaluate the effectiveness of training programs and make adjustments based on feedback and incident data.

Certification: Ensure that employees receive appropriate certifications for safety training and are up-to-date with current standards.

Case Studies in Safety

Case Study 1: Electrical Safety Incident

Scenario: An HVAC technician experienced an electrical shock due to improper grounding of equipment.

Solution: Conducted a review of grounding practices and provided additional training on electrical safety.

Outcome: Improved grounding practices and reduced incidents of electrical shock.

Case Study 2: Refrigerant Leak

Scenario: A refrigerant leak occurred due to improper handling of refrigerant cylinders.

Solution: Implemented stricter handling procedures and provided training on safe refrigerant management.

Outcome: Reduced refrigerant leaks and improved safety in handling procedures.

Case Study 3: Confined Space Safety

Scenario: A technician was injured while working in a confined space without proper PPE.

Solution: Revised safety procedures for confined spaces and provided additional PPE training.

Outcome: Enhanced safety practices and reduced incidents related to confined space work.

Chapter 34: Environmental Regulations

Proper Refrigerant Handling

Importance: Proper refrigerant handling is crucial to prevent environmental damage, health hazards, and legal penalties. Refrigerants can deplete the ozone layer and contribute to global warming if not managed correctly.

Regulations and Guidelines:

EPA Regulations: The U.S. Environmental Protection Agency (EPA) regulates the handling, recovery, and disposal of refrigerants under the Clean Air Act. The rules are designed to minimize emissions and ensure safe practices.

Certification Requirements: Technicians must be certified under Section 608 of the Clean Air Act to handle refrigerants. This certification involves passing an exam on refrigerant handling and safety procedures.

Best Practices:

Leak Detection: Regularly check systems for leaks using electronic leak detectors and repair any issues promptly to prevent refrigerant loss.

Recovery and Recycling: Use recovery machines to capture and recycle refrigerants during servicing and repairs. Ensure proper disposal of refrigerants that cannot be recycled.

Storage: Store refrigerants in labeled, well-ventilated areas and follow manufacturer guidelines for handling and storage.

Energy Efficiency Standards

Purpose: Energy efficiency standards help reduce energy consumption and greenhouse gas emissions, contributing to environmental protection and cost savings for consumers.

Regulatory Bodies: Standards are set by various organizations, including the Department of Energy (DOE) and the American Society of Heating, Refrigerating, and AirConditioning Engineers (ASHRAE).

Key Standards:

SEER and EER Ratings: Seasonal Energy Efficiency Ratio (SEER) and Energy Efficiency Ratio (EER) are metrics used to measure the efficiency of cooling systems. Higher ratings indicate better energy performance.

Furnace Efficiency: Annual Fuel Utilization Efficiency (AFUE) measures the efficiency of heating systems. Modern systems are required to meet minimum AFUE ratings to be considered energy-efficient.

Implementation:

Product Selection: Choose HVAC equipment that meets or exceeds energy efficiency standards. Look for ENERGY STAR® certification, which indicates compliance with high-efficiency criteria.

Building Design: Incorporate energy-efficient practices in building design, such as proper insulation, efficient windows, and advanced HVAC technologies.

EPA Guidelines and Compliance

EPA Role: The EPA enforces regulations aimed at reducing the environmental impact of HVAC systems. This includes overseeing refrigerant management, energy efficiency, and air quality.

Key Regulations:

Refrigerant Management: Compliance with the EPA's refrigerant management program, which includes recovery, recycling, and proper disposal practices.

Energy Efficiency: Adherence to the EPA's energy efficiency programs, including ENERGY STAR® for both equipment and buildings.

Compliance Strategies:

Training: Ensure that all personnel are trained and certified in EPA regulations and guidelines.

Recordkeeping: Maintain detailed records of refrigerant usage, leak repairs, and compliance with energy efficiency standards.

Audits: Conduct regular audits to ensure ongoing compliance with EPA regulations and identify areas for improvement.

Environmental Impact Assessments

Purpose: Environmental impact assessments (EIAs) evaluate the potential effects of HVAC systems on the environment, including energy consumption, emissions, and resource use.

Assessment Process:

PreInstallation Evaluation: Assess the environmental impact of HVAC systems before installation, considering factors such as energy use, refrigerant emissions, and resource requirements.

Ongoing Monitoring: Monitor the environmental performance of installed systems to ensure they operate within acceptable limits and comply with regulations.

Mitigation Measures:

Energy Efficiency Improvements: Implement measures to reduce energy consumption, such as upgrading to high-efficiency equipment and optimizing system performance.

Refrigerant Management: Follow best practices for refrigerant handling and recovery to minimize environmental impact.

Sustainable HVAC Practices

Goal: Sustainable HVAC practices aim to reduce the environmental footprint of HVAC systems by focusing on energy efficiency, renewable energy, and resource conservation.

Practices:

Renewable Energy Integration: Incorporate renewable energy sources, such as solar or geothermal, into HVAC systems to reduce reliance on fossil fuels.

Energy Recovery Systems: Use energy recovery ventilators (ERVs) or heat recovery ventilators (HRVs) to capture and reuse energy from exhaust air.

Green Building Techniques: Implement green building techniques, such as advanced insulation, high-performance windows, and efficient lighting, to complement HVAC systems.

Benefits:

Cost Savings: Sustainable practices can lead to significant cost savings through reduced energy consumption and lower utility bills.

Environmental Protection: Reducing energy use and emissions contributes to environmental conservation and improved air quality.

Green Building Certifications

Purpose: Green building certifications recognize buildings and systems that meet high standards for environmental performance and sustainability.

Certifications:

LEED (Leadership in Energy and Environmental Design): A widely recognized certification program that evaluates buildings based on energy efficiency, water use, indoor environmental quality, and sustainable site development.

BREEAM (Building Research Establishment Environmental Assessment Method): An international certification that assesses building performance in areas such as energy, water, and materials.

Certification Process:

Assessment: Conduct a thorough assessment of the building's HVAC system and overall design to ensure it meets certification criteria.

Documentation: Prepare and submit detailed documentation to the certification body, demonstrating compliance with required standards.

Benefits:

Recognition: Achieving certification enhances the building's marketability and reputation as a sustainable and environmentally friendly project.

Operational Efficiency: Certified buildings often experience improved operational efficiency and reduced environmental impact.

Case Studies in Environmental Compliance

Case Study 1: Refrigerant Management

Scenario: An HVAC company implemented a comprehensive refrigerant management program to comply with EPA regulations.

Solution: Introduced regular leak inspections, staff training, and proper refrigerant recovery and recycling practices.

Outcome: Reduced refrigerant emissions and improved compliance with environmental regulations.

Case Study 2: Energy Efficiency Upgrade

Scenario: A commercial building upgraded its HVAC system to achieve higher energy efficiency and reduce operational costs.

Solution: Installed ENERGY STAR® certified equipment, improved insulation, and integrated renewable energy sources.

Outcome: Significant reduction in energy consumption and utility bills, along with improved environmental performance.

Case Study 3: Green Building Certification

Scenario: A new office building sought LEED certification for its HVAC system and overall design.

Solution: Implemented sustainable HVAC practices, including energy recovery systems and high-efficiency equipment.

Outcome: Achieved LEED certification and enhanced the building's reputation as a sustainable and energy-efficient facility.

Chapter 35: HVAC Certification and Licensing

Obtaining HVAC Certifications

Purpose: HVAC certifications demonstrate a technician's expertise and competence in handling HVAC systems. They are essential for career development and compliance with industry standards.

Certification Bodies: Various organizations offer certifications, including the Environmental Protection Agency (EPA), North American Technician Excellence (NATE), and the Refrigeration Service Engineers Society (RSES).

Common Certifications:

EPA Section 608 Certification: Required for handling refrigerants. It covers various levels, including Type I (small appliances), Type II (high-pressure appliances), and Type III (low-pressure appliances).

NATE Certification: Offers a range of certifications for HVAC technicians, including service, installation, and efficiency analysis.

RSES Certification: Provides comprehensive training and certification for refrigeration and HVAC technicians.

Certification Process:

Application: Apply to the certifying body, often including proof of experience and education.

Examination: Pass a written and/or practical exam that tests knowledge and skills relevant to HVAC systems.

Renewal: Certifications typically require periodic renewal through continuing education or reexamination.

Licensing Requirements by State

Purpose: Licensing ensures that HVAC professionals meet specific regulations and standards. It helps maintain safety, quality, and compliance across the industry.

Variability: Licensing requirements vary by state, including different levels of licensing, application processes, and renewal procedures.

Common Requirements:

Experience and Education: Most states require a certain amount of work experience and/or formal education in HVAC technology.

Examinations: Many states require passing a state-specific licensing exam that covers local codes, regulations, and technical knowledge.

Insurance: Proof of liability insurance may be required to obtain and maintain a license.

State Specific Examples:

California: Requires passing the California State License Board (CSLB) exam and meeting experience requirements. Technicians must also obtain a license for refrigeration.

Texas: Requires passing the Texas Department of Licensing and Regulation (TDLR) exam and meeting experience criteria. Continuing education is required for license renewal.

Continuing Education Opportunities

Purpose: Continuing education helps HVAC professionals stay current with industry trends, technology advancements, and regulatory changes. It is essential for maintaining certifications and licenses.

Formats: Continuing education can include workshops, online courses, seminars, and industry conferences.

Key Areas of Focus:

New Technologies: Stay updated on emerging technologies such as smart HVAC systems and advanced controls.

Regulatory Changes: Learn about updates to building codes, environmental regulations, and safety standards.

Skills Enhancement: Improve practical skills and knowledge in areas such as troubleshooting, installation, and system design.

Sources:

Industry Associations: Many associations, such as NATE and RSES, offer continuing education opportunities and professional development resources.

Technical Schools: Vocational and technical schools provide specialized courses and training programs.

Online Platforms: Online learning platforms offer flexible options for completing continuing education requirements.

Certification Exam Preparation

Purpose: Proper preparation for certification exams is crucial for passing and obtaining credentials. It involves studying relevant materials, practicing test-taking strategies, and gaining hands-on experience.

Resources: Various resources are available to aid in exam preparation, including study guides, practice tests, and preparatory courses.

Preparation Strategies:

Study Guides: Use official study guides provided by certifying bodies or third-party publishers to review exam topics and practice questions.

Practice Tests: Take practice exams to familiarize yourself with the test format and identify areas for improvement.

Hands-on Training: Gain practical experience through apprenticeships or hands-on training programs to reinforce theoretical knowledge.

Support:

Study Groups: Join study groups or forums to discuss exam content and share insights with peers.

Tutors: Consider hiring a tutor or attending preparatory courses if additional help is needed.

Professional Development

Purpose: Professional development involves activities that enhance a technician's skills, knowledge, and career prospects. It supports career growth and keeps professionals competitive in the industry.

Activities: Includes attending industry events, participating in workshops, and pursuing advanced certifications.

Opportunities:

Leadership Training: Develop skills in management, project coordination, and team leadership.

Specialized Certifications: Pursue additional certifications in niche areas such as energy efficiency, green technologies, or advanced diagnostics.

Benefits:

Career Advancement: Enhances job prospects, increases earning potential, and opens opportunities for career progression.

Industry Recognition: Demonstrates commitment to the profession and helps build a professional reputation.

Impact on Career Advancement

Purpose: Certification and licensing have a significant impact on career advancement, affecting job opportunities, salary potential, and professional credibility.

Career Benefits: Certification and licensing can lead to higher-level positions, increased responsibilities, and improved job security.

Effects:

Job Opportunities: Certified and licensed professionals often have access to a broader range of job opportunities and higher-level positions.

Salary Potential: Certifications can lead to higher wages and better compensation packages.

Professional Reputation: Credentials enhance credibility and demonstrate expertise to employers and clients.

Case Studies in Certification

Case Study 1: Advancing Through Certification

Scenario: A technician obtained NATE certification to advance their career in HVAC service.

Solution: The technician completed the certification process, including exam preparation and passing the test.

Outcome: Achieved a promotion to a senior technician role with increased responsibilities and higher salary.

Case Study 2: Navigating State Licensing Requirements

Scenario: An HVAC professional moved to a new state and needed to obtain a local license.

Solution: The professional researched state-specific requirements, completed necessary exams, and provided proof of experience.

Outcome: Successfully obtained the license and continued working in the new state without interruption.

Case Study 3: Enhancing Skills Through Continuing Education

Scenario: A technician enrolled in a continuing education course to learn about new HVAC technologies.

Solution: Completed the course, including practical exercises and theoretical training.

Outcome: Applied new knowledge to improve system installations and troubleshoot complex issues, leading to increased client satisfaction and business growth.

Chapter 36: Starting and Running an HVAC Business

Business Planning Essentials

Purpose: A solid business plan is crucial for launching and managing a successful HVAC business. It outlines the business goals, strategies, and operational plans.

Components: A comprehensive business plan includes market analysis, financial projections, and operational strategies.

Key Elements:

Executive Summary: A snapshot of the business idea, mission statement, and key objectives.

Market Analysis: Research on the local HVAC market, including competition, customer needs, and industry trends.

Business Model: Definition of the business structure (e.g., sole proprietorship, partnership, LLC), services offered, and revenue streams.

Marketing Plan: Strategies for promoting the business, including branding, advertising, and digital presence.

Financial Projections: Budgeting, cash flow forecasts, and financial goals to ensure profitability and sustainability.

Tips:

Research Thoroughly: Understand the local market and competition before finalizing your business plan.

Seek Professional Advice: Consult with business advisors or mentors to refine your plan and address potential challenges.

Marketing and Sales Strategies

Purpose: Effective marketing and sales strategies are essential for attracting customers and growing the HVAC business.

Approach: Use a combination of online and offline marketing techniques to reach potential clients.

Strategies:

Digital Marketing: Utilize SEO, social media, and online advertising to increase visibility and attract leads.

Local Advertising: Invest in local advertising methods such as flyers, local newspaper ads, and sponsorships of community events.

Referral Programs: Encourage satisfied customers to refer others by offering incentives or discounts.

Customer Reviews: Collect and showcase positive customer reviews and testimonials to build credibility and trust.

Sales Tactics:

Consultative Selling: Focus on understanding customer needs and providing tailored solutions.

Effective Follow-Up: Implement a system for following up with leads and closing sales.

Training Sales Team: Train employees on sales techniques, product knowledge, and customer service skills.

Tips:

Track Results: Monitor the effectiveness of marketing campaigns and adjust strategies based on performance data.

Build Relationships: Develop strong relationships with clients to foster loyalty and repeat business.

Managing Operations Effectively

Purpose: Efficient management of operations ensures smooth business processes, high-quality service delivery, and customer satisfaction.

Components: Operational management involves scheduling, inventory management, and quality control.

Key Areas:

Scheduling: Implement scheduling software to manage appointments, track job progress, and optimize technician routes.

Inventory Management: Maintain an organized inventory of tools, equipment, and spare parts to avoid delays and ensure availability.

Quality Control: Establish standards for service delivery and conduct regular quality checks to ensure consistency.

Tips:

Automate Processes: Use technology to automate routine tasks and improve efficiency.

Monitor Performance: Regularly review operational performance and address any issues promptly.

Financial Management Tips

Purpose: Sound financial management is crucial for the financial health and growth of the HVAC business.

Components: Financial management includes budgeting, accounting, and financial planning.

Key Areas:

Budgeting: Create a detailed budget to track expenses, revenue, and cash flow. Regularly review and adjust the budget as needed.

Accounting: Implement accounting software or hire a professional accountant to manage financial records, invoicing, and tax filings.

Financial Planning: Develop long-term financial goals and strategies for investment, growth, and risk management.

Tips:

Monitor Cash Flow: Keep a close eye on cash flow to ensure the business has enough funds to cover expenses and invest in growth.

Plan for Taxes: Set aside funds for taxes and consult with a tax advisor to optimize tax planning and compliance.

Customer Relationship Management

Purpose: Effective customer relationship management (CRM) enhances customer satisfaction, retention, and loyalty.

Components: CRM involves managing customer interactions, feedback, and service quality.

Key Areas:

CRM Software: Use CRM software to track customer interactions, manage appointments, and store customer information.

Customer Feedback: Regularly collect and analyze customer feedback to improve services and address any issues.

Loyalty Programs: Implement loyalty programs or rewards for repeat customers to encourage ongoing business.

Tips:

Personalize Interactions: Tailor communication and service to meet individual customer needs and preferences.

Resolve Issues Promptly: Address customer complaints and issues quickly to maintain satisfaction and trust.

Hiring and Training Employees

Purpose: Hiring and training the right employees is critical for delivering high-quality HVAC services and maintaining a positive work environment.

Components: Recruitment, training, and employee development.

Key Areas:

Recruitment: Develop a recruitment process to attract qualified candidates, including job postings, interviews, and background checks.

Training: Provide comprehensive training on HVAC systems, safety procedures, and customer service to ensure employees are well-prepared.

Employee Development: Offer opportunities for professional growth and advancement to retain top talent and enhance job satisfaction.

Tips:

Foster a Positive Work Culture: Create a supportive and collaborative work environment to boost employee morale and productivity.

Evaluate Performance: Conduct regular performance reviews to provide feedback and identify areas for improvement.

Case Studies in HVAC Business Success

Case Study 1: Growing Through Strategic Marketing

Scenario: An HVAC business implemented a targeted digital marketing campaign to increase visibility and attract new customers.

Solution: Utilized SEO, social media advertising, and local online ads to reach potential clients.

Outcome: Achieved a significant increase in website traffic and lead generation, resulting in higher sales and business growth.

Case Study 2: Streamlining Operations for Efficiency

Scenario: A business adopted scheduling and inventory management software to improve operational efficiency.

Solution: Implemented automated scheduling, real-time inventory tracking, and quality control measures.

Outcome: Reduced operational costs, improved service delivery, and enhanced customer satisfaction.

Case Study 3: Building a Strong Customer Base

Scenario: An HVAC company focused on exceptional customer service and building long-term relationships with clients.

Solution: Implemented a CRM system, collected customer feedback, and launched a referral program.

Outcome: Increased customer retention, generated repeat business, and gained positive referrals.

Book 9:

Specialized HVAC Applications and Indoor Air Quality

Chapter 37: Adapting HVAC for Different Climates

Systems for Cold Climates

Purpose: HVAC systems in cold climates need to be optimized for heating efficiency and frost protection.

Challenges: Extreme cold temperatures, increased heating demands, and potential for equipment freezing.

Key Considerations:

Heating Systems: Use high-efficiency furnaces or boilers capable of handling low temperatures. Consider dual-fuel systems that switch between gas and electric heating based on efficiency.

Insulation: Ensure adequate insulation in walls, roofs, and floors to minimize heat loss. Use thermal breaks and high-value insulation materials.

Ventilation: Implement balanced ventilation systems with heat recovery to prevent heat loss while maintaining indoor air quality.

Pipe Protection: Insulate pipes and ensure proper installation to prevent freezing. Use freeze protection systems where necessary.

Examples: Cold Climate Heat Pumps: Heat pumps designed for low temperatures, such as airsource heat pumps with enhanced defrost capabilities.

Boiler Systems: Condensing boilers that operate efficiently in cold conditions, providing consistent heat output.

Solutions for Hot Climates

Purpose: HVAC systems in hot climates focus on cooling efficiency and managing high heat loads.

Challenges: High outdoor temperatures, increased cooling demands, and potential for high energy costs.

Key Considerations:

Cooling Systems: Use high-efficiency air conditioners or evaporative coolers to handle high heat loads. Consider the use of variable refrigerant flow (VRF) systems for precise temperature control.

Shading and Ventilation: Incorporate shading devices, such as awnings and shades, to reduce solar heat gain. Use natural ventilation strategies to enhance cooling.

Insulation: Ensure proper insulation to keep indoor spaces cool and reduce cooling loads. Use reflective materials to minimize heat absorption.

Examples: Evaporative Coolers: Systems that use the evaporation of water to cool air, suitable for dry climates.

High SEER Air Conditioners: Air conditioners with high Seasonal Energy Efficiency Ratio (SEER) ratings to reduce energy consumption.

HVAC in Humid Climates

Purpose: In humid climates, HVAC systems need to manage both temperature and humidity levels effectively.

Challenges: High humidity can lead to discomfort, mold growth, and increased cooling loads.

Key Considerations:

Dehumidification: Use air conditioners with built-in dehumidification capabilities or dedicated dehumidifiers to control indoor humidity levels.

Ventilation: Implement ventilation systems with humidity control, such as energy recovery ventilators (ERVs) or heat recovery ventilators (HRVs).

Air Quality: Ensure proper air filtration to remove airborne moisture and contaminants. Use moisture-resistant materials to prevent mold growth.

Examples: Variable Air Volume (VAV) Systems: Systems that adjust airflow based on cooling demand, helping manage humidity effectively.

Dedicated Dehumidification Units: Equipment designed specifically for dehumidification, integrated with HVAC systems.

Mixed Climate Solutions

Purpose: Mixed climates experience a range of temperatures and humidity levels, requiring versatile HVAC solutions.

Challenges: Balancing heating and cooling needs, and managing varying humidity levels.

Key Considerations:

Hybrid Systems: Use systems that combine heating and cooling capabilities, such as heat pumps with auxiliary heating options.

Adjustable Controls: Implement programmable thermostats and zoning systems to adapt to changing climate conditions throughout the year.

Energy Efficiency: Choose systems with variable speed motors and high-efficiency ratings to handle fluctuating climate demands.

Examples: DualFuel Heat Pumps: Systems that use heat pumps for cooling and switch to gas or electric heating as needed.

MultiZone Systems: HVAC systems that provide different temperature controls for various zones within the building.

Seasonal Adjustments

Purpose: Seasonal adjustments help optimize HVAC system performance and energy efficiency throughout the year.

Challenges: Adapting systems to changing temperatures and weather conditions.

Key Considerations:

System Maintenance: Perform seasonal maintenance checks to ensure systems are operating efficiently. Clean filters, check refrigerant levels, and inspect heating elements.

Programmable Thermostats: Use programmable or smart thermostats to adjust settings based on seasonal changes and occupancy patterns.

Energy-Saving Tips: Implement energy-saving practices, such as adjusting thermostat settings and sealing leaks, to improve efficiency.

Examples: Seasonal Service Plans: Scheduled maintenance plans that include preseason inspections and adjustments.

Thermostat Programming: Setting thermostats to automatically adjust temperatures based on the time of year.

Climate Specific Components

Purpose: Incorporate components designed to address specific climate challenges and enhance system performance.

Challenges: Ensuring compatibility and effectiveness of climate-specific components.

Key Considerations:

Heating Components: Use components such as frost-resistant heat exchangers and outdoor units with enhanced cold-weather performance.

Cooling Components: Install components like high-efficiency evaporators and condensers for hot climates.

Humidity Control: Implement humidity control systems such as dehumidifiers and humidistats for humid climates.

Examples: Cold Climate Heat Exchangers: Heat exchangers designed for efficient operation in low temperatures.

High-Temperature Condensers: Condensers engineered to handle high heat loads in hot climates.

Case Studies in Climate Adaptation

Case Study 1: HVAC System for a Cold Climate Home

Scenario: Installation of a high-efficiency furnace and pipe insulation in a home located in a region with extreme winter temperatures.

Solution: Use a dual fuel heating system to provide efficient heating and prevent pipe freezing.

Outcome: Improved heating performance and reduced energy costs during winter.

Case Study 2: Cooling Solutions for a Hot Climate Office

Scenario: Installation of high SEER air conditioners and shading devices in an office building in a hot, dry climate.

Solution: Implemented evaporative cooling and reflective insulation to manage high cooling loads.

Outcome: Enhanced indoor comfort and reduced cooling expenses.

Case Study 3: Humidity Control in a Coastal Residence

Scenario: Installation of a dedicated dehumidification unit and ERV system in a coastal home with high humidity levels.

Solution: Used advanced dehumidification and ventilation technologies to manage indoor humidity.

Outcome: Reduced mold growth and improved indoor air quality.

Scan the Qr code to get 11 additional and more detailed topics on:

HVAC Mastering Essentials:
Key insights into careers, technology, maintenance and future trends

Chapter 38: Indoor Air Quality (IAQ) Management

Importance of IAQ

Definition: Indoor Air Quality (IAQ) refers to the condition of air within buildings and its impact on the health and comfort of occupants.

Significance: Good IAQ is crucial for maintaining health, enhancing productivity, and ensuring overall comfort. Poor IAQ can lead to various health issues, including respiratory problems, allergies, and exacerbation of existing conditions.

Health Impacts:

Short-Term Effects: Symptoms such as headaches, fatigue, eye irritation, and dizziness.

Long-Term Effects: Chronic conditions including asthma, cardiovascular diseases, and other serious health issues.

Economic and Environmental Impact:

Healthcare Costs: Reducing IAQ issues can lower healthcare costs associated with air quality-related illnesses.

Energy Efficiency: Improved IAQ can contribute to better energy efficiency in HVAC systems by reducing the load on air filtration and conditioning.

Managing IAQ Effectively

Goal: Effective IAQ management involves maintaining air quality at levels that ensure health and comfort while optimizing energy efficiency.

Approach: Implementing a comprehensive strategy that includes regular monitoring, maintenance, and use of appropriate technologies.

Key Steps:

Assessment: Conduct an IAQ assessment to identify potential sources of contaminants and evaluate current air quality.

Action Plan: Develop and implement an action plan based on assessment results, focusing on both immediate and long-term improvements.

Regular Maintenance: Schedule regular maintenance of HVAC systems to ensure they are functioning correctly and efficiently.

Identifying Common Contaminants

Types of Contaminants: Indoor air can be polluted by various contaminants, including biological, chemical, and particulate matter.

Common Contaminants:

Biological Contaminants: Mold, bacteria, viruses, and pollen. These can cause respiratory issues and other health problems.

Chemical Contaminants: Volatile Organic Compounds (VOCs), formaldehyde, and other off-gassing substances from building materials, cleaning agents, and furnishings.

Particulate Matter: Dust, smoke, and soot that can irritate the respiratory system and contribute to chronic health conditions.

Sources:

Indoor Sources: Household products, cooking, heating, and ventilation systems.

Outdoor Sources: Pollutants from outside that can enter through ventilation systems and windows.

Strategies for IAQ Improvement

Objective: Implement strategies to reduce or eliminate sources of contaminants and improve overall air quality.

Effective Strategies:

Ventilation: Ensure adequate ventilation to dilute and remove indoor pollutants. Use mechanical ventilation systems, such as HRVs and ERVs, to enhance air exchange.

Air Filtration: Use high-efficiency filters (HEPA filters) in HVAC systems to capture airborne particles and allergens.

Source Control: Minimize the use of products that release VOCs and ensure proper storage and disposal of chemicals.

Humidity Control: Maintain optimal indoor humidity levels (3050%) to prevent mold growth and control dust mites.

Regular Cleaning: Implement a regular cleaning schedule to reduce dust, mold, and other contaminants.

Monitoring IAQ

Importance: Regular monitoring helps detect and address IAQ issues before they become significant problems.

Monitoring Techniques:

Air Quality Sensors: Use sensors to measure levels of pollutants, temperature, humidity, and other air quality indicators.

Periodic Testing: Conduct periodic IAQ tests to evaluate the effectiveness of implemented strategies and make necessary adjustments.

Data Logging: Utilize data loggers to track and analyze air quality trends over time.

Tools:

Particulate Matter Meters: Measure concentrations of dust and other particulate pollutants.

Gas Detectors: Detect levels of harmful gases, such as CO_2, CO, and VOCs.

IAQ Technologies

Advancements: Modern technologies offer solutions for enhancing indoor air quality and addressing specific contaminants.

Key Technologies:
Air Purifiers: Devices that remove contaminants from the air using filters, electrostatic charges, or UV light.
Humidity Controllers: Devices and systems designed to regulate indoor humidity levels to prevent mold and improve comfort.
Advanced Filtration Systems: High-efficiency filters and ultraviolet (UV) light systems for air purification.
Air Quality Monitors: Real-time monitoring systems that provide data on various air quality parameters.

Integration:
Smart IAQ Systems: Systems that integrate with smart home technologies to automatically adjust air quality settings based on real-time data.
Building Management Systems: Centralized systems that monitor and control various aspects of building environments, including IAQ.

Case Studies in IAQ Management

Case Study 1: Residential IAQ Improvement
Scenario: Home with persistent mold issues and high humidity levels.
Solution: Installed a whole-house dehumidifier, upgraded air filters to HEPA, and improved ventilation with an ERV system.
Outcome: Reduced mold growth, improved indoor air quality, and enhanced occupant comfort.

Case Study 2: Office Building Air Quality Enhancement
Scenario: Office building experiencing high levels of VOCs from new furnishings and cleaning products.
Solution: Implemented an advanced air purification system with activated carbon filters and increased ventilation rates.
Outcome: Decreased VOC levels, improved employee health, and increased productivity.

Case Study 3: School Air Quality Management
Scenario: School facing high levels of dust and airborne allergens.
Solution: Installed high-efficiency air filters, increased cleaning frequency, and implemented a regular IAQ monitoring program.
Outcome: Improved air quality, reduced absenteeism due to respiratory issues, and enhanced learning environment.

Chapter 39: HVAC in Specialized Settings

Commercial HVAC Systems

Definition: Commercial HVAC systems are designed for larger buildings such as offices, retail spaces, and warehouses. They handle higher loads and often have more complex requirements compared to residential systems.

Components: Typically include larger and more robust heating, cooling, and ventilation equipment.

Key Features:

Scalability: Designed to accommodate the varying needs of different commercial spaces.

Efficiency: Often includes energy-efficient systems to handle high usage and reduce operational costs.

Control Systems: Advanced controls and automation for managing large-scale systems and ensuring consistent performance.

Challenges: Load Variations: Managing different loads and occupancy levels throughout the day.

Space Constraints: Installing and maintaining equipment in confined or multitenant spaces.

Industrial HVAC Solutions

Definition: Industrial HVAC systems cater to manufacturing plants, warehouses, and large production facilities where environmental control is crucial for operations.

Components: Includes heavy-duty systems capable of managing large volumes of air and extreme temperatures.

Key Features:

Durability: Designed to withstand harsh conditions and continuous operation.

Customizability: Often requires custom solutions to meet specific industrial processes and requirements.

Ventilation: Focuses on controlling industrial pollutants, maintaining temperature, and ensuring worker safety.

Challenges: Process Integration: Integrating HVAC systems with manufacturing processes.

Maintenance: Managing the complexity and scale of systems for minimal downtime.

HVAC for Healthcare Facilities

Definition: HVAC systems in healthcare facilities, such as hospitals and clinics, are designed to ensure a controlled environment crucial for patient health and comfort.

Components: Includes specialized equipment for infection control, temperature regulation, and humidity control.

Key Features:

Air Filtration: High-efficiency filters to remove airborne pathogens and particulates.

Temperature and Humidity Control: Strict controls to maintain ideal conditions for patient care and medical equipment.

Isolation Rooms: Specialized systems for isolation rooms and operating theaters to prevent contamination.
Challenges: Infection Control: Meeting stringent infection control standards and regulations.
Redundancy: Ensuring system reliability with backup systems to maintain operations during emergencies.

HVAC in Hospitality

Definition: HVAC systems in hotels, resorts, and other hospitality venues focus on providing comfort and optimizing energy efficiency while enhancing guest experiences.
Components: Includes climate control systems for guest rooms, public areas, and service spaces.
Key Features:
Guest Comfort: Systems designed to provide individualized comfort controls in guest rooms.
Energy Management: Implementing energy-efficient systems to reduce operational costs while maintaining comfort.
Noise Control: Minimizing noise from HVAC systems to enhance guest experiences.
Challenges: High Turnover: Managing HVAC needs with frequent guest turnover and varying occupancy levels.
Integration: Integrating HVAC systems with building management systems and guest services.

Data Center HVAC Requirements

Definition: Data centers require specialized HVAC systems to ensure optimal operating conditions for servers and IT equipment.
Components: Includes cooling systems designed to handle high heat loads and maintain precise temperature controls.
Key Features:
Cooling Systems: Precision cooling systems to handle high heat loads from IT equipment.
Redundancy: Implementing redundant systems to ensure continuous operation and prevent downtime.
Monitoring: Advanced monitoring systems for real-time tracking of temperature, humidity, and equipment status.
Challenges: Heat Management: Managing the high heat generated by servers and other IT equipment.
Energy Consumption: Addressing the high energy consumption and implementing energy-efficient solutions.

HVAC for Educational Institutions

Definition: HVAC systems in schools, colleges, and universities focus on providing a comfortable learning environment while accommodating varying occupancy levels and activities.
Components: Includes systems for classrooms, auditoriums, gyms, and administrative offices.
Key Features:
Comfort: Ensuring optimal temperature and air quality in learning environments.

Flexibility: Systems designed to adapt to varying schedules and occupancy levels.

Energy Efficiency: Implementing energy-efficient solutions to manage operational costs and environmental impact.

Challenges: Scheduling: Managing HVAC needs with varying schedules and seasonal changes.

Maintenance: Ensuring reliable operation with minimal disruption to educational activities.

Case Studies in Specialized HVAC

Case Study 1: Commercial Office Building

Scenario: Large office building with varying occupancy and load requirements.

Solution: Implemented a variable refrigerant flow (VRF) system with advanced controls and energy-efficient components.

Outcome: Improved comfort, reduced energy consumption, and enhanced system flexibility.

Case Study 2: Industrial Manufacturing Plant

Scenario: Manufacturing plant requiring precise temperature and humidity control for production processes.

Solution: Installed custom HVAC systems with robust filtration and high-capacity cooling units.

Outcome: Enhanced operational efficiency, reduced downtime, and maintained optimal production conditions.

Case Study 3: Healthcare Facility

Scenario: Hospital requiring stringent infection control and temperature regulation.

Solution: Implemented high-efficiency air filtration systems, temperature and humidity controls, and backup systems for critical areas.

Outcome: Improved patient safety, enhanced comfort, and ensured compliance with health regulations.

Case Study 4: Hospitality Venue

Scenario: Luxury hotel with high guest turnover and varying occupancy levels.

Solution: Integrated smart HVAC systems with individual room controls and energy management features.

Outcome: Enhanced guest comfort, reduced operational costs, and improved energy efficiency.

Case Study 5: Data Center

Scenario: Data center with high heat loads and critical cooling requirements.

Solution: Installed precision cooling systems with redundant backup and real-time monitoring.

Outcome: Maintained optimal operating conditions, prevented downtime, and improved energy efficiency.

Case Study 6: Educational Institution

Scenario: University campus with diverse HVAC needs for classrooms and common areas.

Solution: Implemented zoned HVAC systems with programmable controls and energy-efficient components.

Outcome: Improved comfort, reduced energy costs, and adapted to varying occupancy levels.

Book 10:

The Future of HVAC and Real-world Case Studies

Chapter 40: Innovations and Emerging Technologies

IoT and Smart HVAC Systems

Definition: The Internet of Things (IoT) refers to interconnected devices that communicate and share data over the Internet. Smart HVAC systems leverage IoT to enhance control, efficiency, and user experience.

Components: Includes smart thermostats, sensors, and remote monitoring tools.

Key Features:

Remote Access: Allows users to control HVAC systems remotely via smartphones or computers.

Data Analytics: Provides insights into system performance, energy usage, and maintenance needs.

Automation: Automates system adjustments based on user preferences and environmental conditions.

Benefits:

Energy Efficiency: Optimizes energy usage by adjusting settings based on occupancy and weather conditions.

Convenience: Offers remote management and real-time alerts for system issues.

Cost Savings: Reduces operational costs through efficient energy management and predictive maintenance.

Challenges: Security: Ensuring data privacy and protection against cyber threats.

Integration: Integrating new technologies with existing systems and infrastructure.

Integrating Renewable Energy

Definition: Incorporating renewable energy sources, such as solar, wind, and geothermal, into HVAC systems to reduce reliance on fossil fuels and lower environmental impact.

Components: Includes solar panels, wind turbines, and geothermal heat pumps.

Key Features:

Sustainable Energy: Utilizes renewable sources to power HVAC systems, reducing carbon footprint.

Energy Independence: Reduces dependency on grid electricity and enhances energy security.

Cost Savings: Offers long-term savings through reduced energy bills and potential incentives.

Benefits:

Environmental Impact: Decreases greenhouse gas emissions and promotes sustainability.

Economic Incentives: Provides opportunities for tax credits, rebates, and other financial benefits.

Energy Reliability: Enhances system reliability and resilience.

Challenges: Initial Costs: Higher upfront costs for renewable energy systems and installation.

Intermittency: Managing energy supply and demand due to variable renewable sources.

AI and Machine Learning in HVAC

Definition: Artificial Intelligence (AI) and Machine Learning (ML) involve the use of algorithms and data to improve system performance, predict failures, and optimize operations.

Components: Includes AI-driven control systems, predictive analytics, and automated diagnostics.

Key Features:

Predictive Maintenance: Uses data to anticipate and prevent system failures before they occur.

Performance Optimization: Continuously adjusts settings for optimal efficiency and comfort.

DataDriven Insights: Analyzes large volumes of data to identify patterns and make informed decisions.

Benefits:

Operational Efficiency: Enhances system performance and reduces energy consumption.

Reduced Downtime: Minimizes unexpected failures and maintenance issues.

Improved User Experience: Provides personalized comfort and convenience based on user preferences.

Challenges: Complexity: Requires sophisticated algorithms and substantial data to function effectively.

Data Privacy: Ensures that data collected and used by AI systems is secure and private.

Advanced Materials and Components

Definition: The development of new materials and components that improve HVAC system performance, durability, and efficiency.

Components: Includes advanced heat exchangers, high-efficiency filters, and smart insulation materials.

Key Features:

Enhanced Performance: Materials designed for better heat transfer, reduced energy loss, and improved durability.

Sustainability: Use of eco-friendly materials that contribute to greener building practices.

Innovation: Ongoing research and development in material science to address HVAC challenges.

Benefits:

Energy Efficiency: Improves system efficiency and reduces energy consumption.

Longevity: Extends the lifespan of HVAC components and systems.

Environmental Impact: Reduces environmental impact through the use of sustainable materials.

Challenges: Cost: Higher costs for advanced materials and components.

Integration: Ensuring compatibility with existing HVAC systems and technologies.

Predictive Maintenance Technologies

Definition: Technologies that use data and analytics to predict and address maintenance needs before issues arise.

Components: Includes sensors, data analytics platforms, and diagnostic tools.

Key Features:

RealTime Monitoring: Tracks system performance and identifies potential issues in real-time.

Data Analysis: Analyzes data to predict maintenance needs and optimize scheduling.

Proactive Approach: Shifts from reactive maintenance to proactive management.

Benefits:
Reduced Downtime: Minimizes unexpected failures and system interruptions.
Cost Savings: Reduces maintenance costs by addressing issues early.
Enhanced Reliability: Improves system reliability and performance.
Challenges: Data Management: Requires effective data collection and analysis capabilities.
Implementation: Integrating predictive maintenance technologies with existing systems.

Future HVAC System Designs

Definition: Emerging HVAC system designs that incorporate new technologies, materials, and approaches to meet evolving needs and challenges.
Components: Includes modular systems, hybrid solutions, and advanced control strategies.
Key Features:
Flexibility: Modular designs that can be easily adapted to changing requirements and technologies.
Integration: Combining various technologies and systems for optimized performance.
Sustainability: Emphasis on energy efficiency, renewable energy integration, and reduced environmental impact.
Benefits:
Adaptability: Provides solutions that can evolve with technological advancements and changing needs.
Efficiency: Enhances system performance and energy efficiency.
Innovation: Encourages the development of cutting-edge solutions and technologies.
Challenges: Cost: Higher costs for research, development, and implementation of new designs.
Integration: Ensuring compatibility and seamless integration with existing systems.

Case Studies in Innovation

Case Study 1: IoTEnabled Smart HVAC System
Scenario: A commercial building implemented an IoT-enabled HVAC system for enhanced control and efficiency.
Solution: Integrated smart thermostats, sensors, and remote monitoring tools.
Outcome: Improved energy efficiency, reduced operational costs, and enhanced user experience through remote management and real-time data.

Case Study 2: Renewable Energy Integration in a Residential HVAC System
Scenario: A residential property integrated solar panels with its HVAC system to reduce reliance on grid electricity.
Solution: Installed solar panels, connected to a high-efficiency heat pump and energy storage system.
Outcome: Achieved significant energy savings, reduced carbon footprint, and enhanced energy independence.

Case Study 3: AIDriven Predictive Maintenance for an Industrial HVAC System
Scenario: An industrial facility implemented AI-driven predictive maintenance technologies for its HVAC system.

Solution: Deployed sensors and data analytics platforms to monitor system performance and predict maintenance needs.

Outcome: Reduced unexpected failures, minimized downtime, and improved system reliability.

Case Study 4: Advanced Materials in Commercial HVAC Systems

Scenario: A commercial building upgraded its HVAC system using advanced materials and components for improved performance.

Solution: Installed high-efficiency heat exchangers, advanced filters, and smart insulation materials.

Outcome: Enhanced system efficiency, reduced energy consumption, and extended component lifespan.

Case Study 5: Future HVAC System Design in a Green Building

Scenario: A new green building project incorporated modular HVAC systems and hybrid solutions for optimized performance.

Solution: Implemented modular HVAC units, hybrid systems combining renewable energy sources, and advanced control strategies.

Outcome: Achieved high energy efficiency, adaptability to changing needs, and minimized environmental impact.

Chapter 41: Sustainable HVAC Practices

Green HVAC Solutions

Definition: Green HVAC solutions aim to minimize environmental impact while maintaining high performance and efficiency. These solutions focus on reducing energy consumption, using renewable energy sources, and lowering emissions.

Components: Includes energy-efficient equipment, renewable energy systems, and advanced control technologies.

Key Features:

Energy Efficiency: Utilizes high-efficiency HVAC systems and components to reduce energy consumption.

Renewable Energy Integration: Incorporates renewable energy sources like solar or geothermal to power HVAC systems.

Reduced Emissions: Focuses on technologies that reduce greenhouse gas emissions and pollutants.

Benefits:

Environmental Impact: Reduces carbon footprint and promotes sustainability.

Cost Savings: Lower energy bills through efficient equipment and renewable energy use.

Enhanced Comfort: Maintains high levels of indoor comfort while minimizing environmental impact.

Challenges:

Initial Costs: Higher upfront costs for green HVAC equipment and technologies.

System Integration: Ensuring compatibility with existing systems and infrastructure.

Strategies for Reducing Carbon Footprint

Definition: Strategies aimed at minimizing the carbon footprint of HVAC systems through energy efficiency, renewable energy, and sustainable practices.

Components: Includes energy audits, equipment upgrades, and process improvements.

Key Strategies:

Energy Audits: Assess energy usage and identify opportunities for improvement.

Upgrading Equipment: Replace outdated systems with high-efficiency models.

Renewable Energy: Integrate solar panels, wind turbines, or other renewable sources.

Benefits:

Reduced Emissions: Lowers greenhouse gas emissions and environmental impact.

Cost Efficiency: Reduces energy costs and improves system performance.

Sustainability: Contributes to overall sustainability goals and initiatives.

Challenges:

Implementation Costs: Costs associated with implementing carbon reduction strategies.

Monitoring and Measurement: Tracking progress and measuring the impact of strategies.

Achieving LEED Certification

Definition: LEED (Leadership in Energy and Environmental Design) certification is a globally recognized rating system for the design, construction, and operation of high-performance green buildings.

Components: Includes prerequisites and credits related to energy efficiency, indoor environmental quality, and sustainable site development.

Key Requirements:

Energy Efficiency: Meet specific energy performance standards and benchmarks.

Sustainable Materials: Use materials and products with low environmental impact.

Indoor Air Quality: Ensure high indoor air quality through effective ventilation and filtration.

Benefits:

Recognition: Achieving LEED certification enhances the building's marketability and credibility.

Operational Savings: Reduced energy and water costs through efficient design and practices.

Environmental Impact: Contributes to environmental sustainability and resource conservation.

Challenges:

Certification Process: Navigating the complex certification process and requirements.

Costs: Costs associated with certification and implementing required measures.

Sustainable Materials and Methods

Definition: Use of eco-friendly materials and construction methods that reduce environmental impact and enhance the sustainability of HVAC systems.

Components: Includes recycled materials, low-emission products, and energy-efficient construction techniques.

Key Materials and Methods:

Recycled Materials: Use of recycled or repurposed materials in HVAC components.

LowEmission Products: Selection of products with low volatile organic compounds (VOCs) and other emissions.

EnergyEfficient Techniques: Employing methods that reduce energy consumption during construction and operation.

Benefits:

Environmental Impact: Reduces resource consumption and waste.

Health and Safety: Improves indoor air quality and occupant health.

Cost Savings: Potential for long-term cost savings through durable and efficient materials.

Challenges:

Availability: Finding and sourcing sustainable materials and products.

Cost: Higher costs for some eco-friendly materials and methods.

Energy Recovery and Reuse

Definition: Technologies and practices that capture and reuse energy from HVAC systems to improve efficiency and reduce waste.

Components: Includes heat recovery ventilators (HRVs), energy recovery ventilators (ERVs), and heat exchangers.

Key Technologies:

HRVs and ERVs: Systems that recover heat from exhausted air and use it to precondition incoming air.

Heat Exchangers: Devices that transfer heat between different fluid streams to maximize energy efficiency.

Waste Heat Utilization: Using waste heat from industrial processes or other sources to power HVAC systems.

Benefits:

Energy Efficiency: Improves overall system efficiency by reusing recovered energy.

Cost Savings: Reduces energy costs through efficient energy use.

Sustainability: Contributes to reducing overall energy consumption and environmental impact.

Challenges:

Initial Costs: Higher initial investment for energy recovery systems.

Integration: Ensuring compatibility with existing HVAC systems and infrastructure.

Water Conservation in HVAC

Definition: Practices and technologies aimed at reducing water usage and waste in HVAC systems.

Components: Includes water-saving equipment, efficient cooling towers, and recycling systems.

Key Practices:

Efficient Cooling Towers: Using water-efficient cooling tower designs and technologies.

Water Recycling Systems: Implementing systems to capture and reuse water in HVAC processes.

Leak Prevention: Regular maintenance and inspections to prevent water leaks and wastage.

Benefits:

Resource Conservation: Reduces water consumption and conserves natural resources.

Cost Savings: Lowers water utility costs and reduces wastewater management expenses.

Sustainability: Contributes to overall environmental sustainability goals.

Challenges:

Implementation: Costs and complexities of installing water-saving technologies.

Maintenance: Ensuring ongoing maintenance and operation of water conservation systems.

Case Studies in Sustainability

Case Study 1: Green HVAC Solutions in a Commercial Building

Scenario: A large office building implemented green HVAC solutions to enhance energy efficiency and reduce environmental impact.

Solution: Integrated high-efficiency HVAC equipment, renewable energy sources, and advanced control systems.

Outcome: Achieved significant energy savings, reduced carbon footprint, and improved occupant comfort.

Case Study 2: Carbon Footprint Reduction in a Residential Property

Scenario: A residential home focused on reducing its carbon footprint through energy-efficient HVAC upgrades and renewable energy integration.

Solution: Upgraded to a high-efficiency heat pump, installed solar panels, and implemented energy-saving strategies.

Outcome: Reduced energy bills, lowered greenhouse gas emissions, and increased energy independence.

Case Study 3: LEED Certification for a New Green Building

Scenario: A new commercial building pursued LEED certification to meet high sustainability standards and enhance marketability.

Solution: Implemented energy-efficient HVAC systems, used sustainable materials, and ensured high indoor air quality.

Outcome: Achieved LEED certification, reduced operational costs, and enhanced building reputation.

Case Study 4: Energy Recovery in an Industrial Facility

Scenario: An industrial facility implemented energy recovery systems to improve efficiency and reduce waste.

Solution: Installed heat recovery ventilators (HRVs) and energy recovery ventilators (ERVs) to capture and reuse energy.

Outcome: Enhanced system efficiency, reduced energy costs, and minimized environmental impact.

Case Study 5: Water Conservation in a Healthcare Facility

Scenario: A healthcare facility focused on water conservation to reduce water usage and waste in its HVAC systems.

Solution: Implement water-efficient cooling towers, recycling systems, and regular maintenance practices.

Outcome: Achieved significant water savings, reduced utility costs, and contributed to environmental sustainability.

Chapter 42: Trends and Future Directions

Industry Market Analysis

Definition: Industry market analysis involves examining current trends, growth factors, and market dynamics within the HVAC sector. It provides insights into market size, key players, and competitive landscape.

Components: Market segmentation, growth drivers, challenges, and emerging opportunities.

Key Aspects:

Market Size and Growth: Overview of the current market size and projected growth rates.

Key Players: Major companies and their market share.

Consumer Demand: Trends in consumer preferences and demands.

Technological Advancements: Innovations driving market growth.

Benefits:

Strategic Planning: Helps businesses make informed decisions and strategic plans.

Investment Opportunities: Identifies potential areas for investment and expansion.

Competitive Advantage: Provides insights into competitors and market positioning.

Challenges: Market Volatility: Adapting to changes and uncertainties in the market.

Regulatory Compliance: Navigating evolving regulations and standards.

Predictions for Future Developments

Definition: Forecasts and predictions about future trends, technological advancements, and market developments in the HVAC industry.

Components: Emerging technologies, market growth projections, and anticipated changes.

Key Predictions:

Technological Innovations: Advancements in HVAC technology, such as smart systems and energy-efficient solutions.

Market Growth: Expected growth in different segments, such as residential, commercial, and industrial HVAC systems.

Consumer Trends: Changes in consumer preferences and demands for sustainable and smart HVAC solutions.

Benefits:

Future Readiness: Helps businesses and professionals prepare for future developments and trends.

Innovation Opportunities: Identifies potential areas for innovation and new product development.

Strategic Positioning: Aids in positioning businesses to capitalize on future market opportunities.

Challenges: Uncertainty: Navigating uncertainties and risks associated with future predictions.

Adaptation: Adapting to rapid changes and advancements in technology.

Smart Building Innovations

Definition: Innovations related to integrating HVAC systems with smart building technologies to enhance efficiency, comfort, and control.

Components: Smart thermostats, building automation systems, and IoT integration.

Key Innovations:

Smart Thermostats: Advanced thermostats with learning capabilities and remote control.

Building Automation Systems: Systems that integrate HVAC, lighting, security, and other building functions.

IoT Integration: Connecting HVAC systems to the Internet of Things (IoT) for real-time monitoring and control.

Benefits:

Enhanced Efficiency: Improved energy efficiency and reduced operational costs.

Increased Comfort: Better control of indoor climate and comfort levels.

Remote Access: Ability to monitor and control systems remotely.

Challenges: Integration: Ensuring compatibility and integration with existing systems.

Security: Addressing cybersecurity concerns related to smart systems.

Global HVAC Market Trends

Definition: Examination of global trends and developments in the HVAC market, including regional differences and international growth.

Components: Market growth, regional trends, and international opportunities.

Key Trends:

Regional Growth: Growth in emerging markets and regions with increasing HVAC demand.

Technological Advancements: Global adoption of new technologies and innovations.

Sustainability Focus: Growing emphasis on sustainable and energy-efficient HVAC solutions.

Benefits:

Global Opportunities: Identifies opportunities for international expansion and market entry.

Competitive Insights: Provides insights into global competitors and market dynamics.

Market Diversification: Helps in diversifying market strategies and offerings.

Challenges: Regulatory Differences: Navigating different regulations and standards in various regions.

Market Competition: Competing in a global market with diverse competitors.

Policy and Regulatory Changes

Definition: Examination of current and anticipated changes in policies and regulations affecting the HVAC industry.

Components: Regulatory standards, environmental policies, and industry-specific regulations.

Key Changes:
Environmental Regulations: New standards for energy efficiency and emissions.
Building Codes: Updates to building codes and standards affecting HVAC design and installation.
Incentives and Rebates: Changes in government incentives and rebates for energy-efficient systems.
Benefits:
Compliance: Helps businesses stay compliant with new regulations and standards.
Opportunities: Identifies opportunities for taking advantage of incentives and rebates.
Risk Management: Aids in managing risks associated with regulatory changes.
Challenges: Adapting to Changes: Keeping up with and adapting to evolving regulations.
Compliance Costs: Managing costs associated with compliance and regulatory requirements.

Future Challenges and Opportunities

Definition: Examination of potential challenges and opportunities facing the HVAC industry in the future.
Components: Market challenges, technological opportunities, and industry trends.
Key Challenges:
Technological Complexity: Managing the complexity of new technologies and innovations.
Regulatory Compliance: Adapting to changing regulations and standards.
Market Competition: Navigating increased competition and market saturation.
Key Opportunities:
Innovation: Opportunities for developing and adopting new technologies.
Sustainability: Growing demand for sustainable and energy-efficient solutions.
Global Expansion: Expanding into emerging markets with increasing HVAC demand.
Benefits:
Strategic Planning: Helps businesses prepare for future challenges and capitalize on opportunities.
Innovation and Growth: Identifies areas for innovation and growth in the industry.
Risk Management: Aids in managing potential risks and uncertainties.

Case Studies in Market Trends
Case Study 1: Adoption of Smart HVAC Systems in Commercial Buildings
Scenario: A commercial building implemented smart HVAC systems to enhance energy efficiency and operational control.
Solution: Integrated advanced thermostats, building automation systems, and IoT technologies.
Outcome: Achieved significant energy savings, improved system performance, and increased tenant satisfaction.
Case Study 2: Global Expansion of HVAC Companies into Emerging Markets
Scenario: An HVAC company expanded its operations into emerging markets with growing HVAC demand.
Solution: Entered new markets with tailored products and strategies to meet regional needs.

Outcome: Increased market share, revenue growth, and expanded global presence.

Case Study 3: Navigating Regulatory Changes in the HVAC Industry

Scenario: An HVAC company adapted to new environmental regulations and building codes.

Solution: Implemented changes to meet regulatory requirements and took advantage of government incentives.

Outcome: Achieved compliance, benefited from incentives, and maintained competitive advantage.

Case Study 4: Addressing Challenges of Technological Complexity

Scenario: An HVAC company faced challenges in integrating new technologies and managing system complexity.

Solution: Develop training programs and support systems to address technological challenges.

Outcome: Improved technology integration, reduced operational issues, and enhanced system performance.

Case Study 5: Opportunities in Sustainable HVAC Solutions

Scenario: A company focused on developing and marketing sustainable HVAC solutions.

Solution: Introduced energy-efficient products, sustainable materials, and green building practices.

Outcome: Gained market recognition, increased sales, and contributed to environmental sustainability.

Chapter 43: Retrofitting and Upgrading HVAC Systems

Assessing Existing Systems

Definition: Evaluating the performance, condition, and efficiency of current HVAC systems to identify areas for improvement or replacement.

Components: System performance, energy consumption, component wear, and operational issues.

Key Steps:

System Inspection: Conduct a thorough inspection of existing HVAC equipment, including heating, cooling, and ventilation components.

Performance Assessment: Evaluate the system's performance metrics, such as efficiency ratings, energy usage, and cooling/heating capacity.

Condition Analysis: Check for signs of wear, damage, or outdated technology.

Compliance Check: Ensure the system meets current codes and standards.

Benefits:

Identify Needs: Pinpoint areas where upgrades or replacements are necessary.

Cost Savings: Determine potential cost savings from improved efficiency and reduced energy consumption.

Enhanced Performance: Improve system reliability and comfort.

Challenges:

Complexity: Dealing with complex systems and integrating new technologies.

Cost: Balancing the cost of assessment with potential benefits.

Planning Effective Retrofits

Definition: Developing a comprehensive plan for updating or replacing existing HVAC systems to enhance performance, efficiency, and compliance.

Components: Retrofit goals, design considerations, and implementation strategies.

Key Steps:

Define Objectives: Set clear goals for the retrofit, such as improving energy efficiency, reducing operating costs, or increasing system capacity.

Design Plan: Create a detailed plan outlining the retrofit process, including equipment selection, system design, and installation procedures.

Budgeting: Estimate costs and identify potential funding sources or financial incentives.

Scheduling: Develop a timeline for the retrofit, including key milestones and deadlines.

Benefits:

Improved Efficiency: Enhance system performance and energy efficiency.

Cost Savings: Reduce operational and maintenance costs.

Enhanced Comfort: Improve indoor climate and comfort levels.

Challenges: Integration: Ensuring new components integrate seamlessly with existing systems.
Disruption: Minimizing disruption during the retrofit process.

Common Retrofit Solutions

Definition: Popular solutions for upgrading or replacing HVAC systems to improve performance, efficiency, and comfort.
Components: Equipment upgrades, technology enhancements, and system modifications.
Common Solutions:
High-Efficiency HVAC Units: Upgrading to energy-efficient heating and cooling systems.
Smart Thermostats: Installing advanced thermostats with learning capabilities and remote control.
Duct Sealing and Insulation: Improving ductwork to reduce energy loss and enhance system efficiency.
Variable Speed Motors: Upgrading to variable speed motors for better control and energy savings.
Air Quality Improvements: Adding air purifiers, dehumidifiers, or ventilation enhancements.
Benefits:
Energy Savings: Lower energy consumption and reduced utility bills.
Increased Comfort: Enhanced indoor climate control and air quality.
System Longevity: Extended lifespan of HVAC equipment.
Challenges: Cost: Balancing the cost of upgrades with potential savings.
Compatibility: Ensuring new solutions are compatible with existing systems.

Exploring Financial Incentives

Definition: Identifying and utilizing financial incentives and rebates to offset the cost of retrofitting or upgrading HVAC systems.
Components: Government programs, utility incentives, and tax credits.
Types of Incentives:
Utility Rebates: Discounts or rebates offered by utility companies for energy-efficient upgrades.
Government Programs: Federal, state, or local programs providing financial assistance for HVAC improvements.
Tax Credits: Tax credits or deductions for installing energy-efficient equipment or making home improvements.
Benefits:
Cost Reduction: Lower upfront costs for retrofitting or upgrading HVAC systems.
Increased Affordability: Make energy-efficient improvements more accessible.
Financial Savings: Long-term savings through reduced energy consumption.
Challenges: Eligibility: Navigating eligibility requirements and application processes.
Availability: Availability of incentives may vary by location and program.

Enhancing Energy Efficiency

Definition: Implementing strategies and technologies to improve the energy efficiency of HVAC systems, reducing energy consumption and operational costs.

Components: Energy-efficient equipment, system upgrades, and performance optimization.

Strategies:

HighEfficiency Equipment: Upgrade to ENERGY STAR® rated HVAC units and components.

Building Insulation: Improve insulation to reduce heat loss and gain.

Optimized Controls: Implement advanced control systems and smart thermostats.

Regular Maintenance: Ensure routine maintenance to keep systems running efficiently.

Benefits:

Cost Savings: Reduced energy bills and operational costs.

Environmental Impact: Lower carbon footprint and reduced environmental impact.

Improved Performance: Enhanced system performance and reliability.

Challenges: Initial Investment: High upfront costs for energy-efficient upgrades.

Technological Complexity: Integrating new technologies with existing systems.

Retrofit Technologies

Definition: Technologies and innovations used in the retrofitting process to upgrade or replace existing HVAC systems.

Components: Equipment, controls, and monitoring technologies.

Technologies:

Smart HVAC Systems: Advanced systems with IoT integration and remote control capabilities.

Energy Recovery Ventilators (ERVs): Systems that recover and reuse energy from exhaust air.

Advanced Filtration Systems: High-efficiency air filters and purification technologies.

DemandControlled Ventilation: Systems that adjust ventilation based on real-time demand and occupancy.

Benefits:

Enhanced Efficiency: Improved energy efficiency and reduced operational costs.

Increased Comfort: Better control of indoor climate and air quality.

FutureProofing: Adoption of technologies that prepare systems for future advancements.

Challenges: Integration: Ensuring compatibility with existing systems and infrastructure.

Training: Training staff to operate and maintain new technologies effectively.

Chapter 44: Software Tools and Case Studies

HVAC Design Software

Definition: Software tools used for designing, modeling, and optimizing HVAC systems to ensure efficiency and compliance with standards.

Components: Features, benefits, and examples of popular HVAC design software.

Key Software Tools:

Auto CAD MEP: Provides comprehensive tools for designing HVAC systems, including ductwork, piping, and equipment layout.

Carrier HAP (Hourly Analysis Program): Facilitates detailed load calculations, energy modeling, and system design.

Trane TRACE 700: Offers advanced simulation and analysis for HVAC system design and energy efficiency.

Rhinoceros + Grasshopper: For custom HVAC modeling and integration with architectural designs.

Benefits:

Accuracy: Enhanced precision in system design and load calculations.

Efficiency: Streamlined design processes and reduced time spent on manual calculations.

Visualization: Improved ability to visualize and modify HVAC designs before implementation.

Challenges:

Complexity: Requires training and expertise to use effectively.

Cost: Some software tools come with significant licensing fees.

Simulation Tools for HVAC

Definition: Tools used to simulate the performance of HVAC systems under various conditions to predict behavior and optimize performance.

Components: Types of simulations, benefits, and examples of simulation tools.

Key Simulation Tools:

EnergyPlus: A powerful simulation engine for modeling building energy and HVAC systems, including heating, cooling, and ventilation.

eQUEST: An easy-to-use tool for energy modeling and simulation, ideal for building performance analysis.

FLOW3D: Used for detailed airflow simulations and analysis of complex HVAC systems.

IES VE (Integrated Environmental Solutions Virtual Environment): Provides a comprehensive suite for building simulation, including HVAC and energy modeling.

Benefits:

Predictive Analysis: Ability to predict system performance and identify potential issues before implementation.

Optimization: Helps optimize system design for energy efficiency and performance.

Cost Savings: Reduces the risk of costly design errors and operational inefficiencies.
Challenges:
Data Requirements: Accurate simulations require detailed input data and accurate models.
Complexity: Advanced simulation tools may have a steep learning curve.

Maintenance Management Software

Definition: Software tools designed to help manage and streamline HVAC maintenance activities, track performance, and schedule tasks.
Components: Features, benefits, and examples of maintenance management software.
Key Software Tools:
CMMS (Computerized Maintenance Management Systems): Tools like Fiix or Hippo that help manage maintenance schedules, track work orders, and maintain equipment records.
eMaint: Provides features for tracking maintenance tasks, managing inventory, and generating reports.
Maintenance Connection: Offers comprehensive tools for managing preventive maintenance, work orders, and asset tracking.
UpKeep: A mobile-friendly CMMS that simplifies maintenance management with task tracking, scheduling, and communication features.
Benefits:
Efficiency: Streamlines maintenance processes and reduces downtime.
Tracking: Improves tracking of maintenance activities and equipment performance.
Cost Management: Helps control maintenance costs and optimize resource allocation.
Challenges:
Implementation: Requires proper setup and integration with existing systems.
Training: Staff may need training to use the software effectively.

Detailed Residential Case Studies

Definition: In-depth analysis of residential HVAC projects, showcasing design, implementation, and performance outcomes.
Components: Examples of successful residential HVAC installations and their results.
Case Studies:
High-Efficiency Home Retrofit: Analysis of a home retrofit project focusing on energy-efficient HVAC upgrades, including new equipment, ductwork improvements, and insulation enhancements.
Smart Home Integration: A case study of a residential HVAC system integrated with smart home technology, including smart thermostats, remote control, and energy monitoring.
Sustainable Design: A project highlighting the use of green HVAC solutions in a residential setting, such as geothermal heat pumps or solar-assisted systems.
Benefits:
RealWorld Insights: Provides practical examples of HVAC system design and performance in residential settings.

Best Practices: Highlights successful strategies and technologies for residential HVAC projects.
Challenges:
Variability: Each case study may have unique challenges and solutions, making it difficult to generalize findings.

Comprehensive Commercial Case Studies

Definition: Detailed analysis of commercial HVAC projects, demonstrating design considerations, implementation strategies, and performance results.

Components: Examples of successful commercial HVAC installations and their outcomes.

Case Studies:

Office Building Retrofit: Analysis of a retrofit project in an office building, focusing on energy efficiency upgrades, system integration, and operational improvements.

Retail Store HVAC System: A case study of a commercial HVAC system designed for a retail environment, including considerations for temperature control, humidity management, and customer comfort.

Hospital HVAC Implementation: Examination of HVAC system design and installation in a healthcare facility, addressing specific requirements for air quality, temperature control, and energy efficiency.

Benefits:

Practical Examples: Provides real-world examples of HVAC system design and performance in commercial settings.

Lessons Learned: Offers insights into common challenges and successful strategies in commercial HVAC projects.

Challenges:

Complexity: Commercial projects often involve complex systems and large-scale considerations.

Industrial HVAC Success Stories
Transforming a High-Tech Data Center's Cooling Efficiency

A prominent tech company in Silicon Valley faced escalating cooling costs and frequent failures in their data center, which housed critical servers generating substantial heat. The outdated HVAC system was struggling to keep pace with the increasing demands of modern data processing.

Solution:

The company undertook a major HVAC overhaul, introducing advanced cooling technologies including high-efficiency chillers and precision air conditioning units. They integrated a sophisticated Building Management System (BMS) to optimize cooling based on real-time server loads and environmental conditions.

Results:

The upgrade led to a dramatic 40% reduction in cooling costs. Downtime due to cooling failures was virtually eliminated, and the lifespan of the servers was extended. The project was completed on time and within budget, demonstrating a successful implementation of cutting-edge HVAC solutions in a high-stakes environment.

Revolutionizing Climate Control in an Automotive Manufacturing Plant

An automotive manufacturing plant in Detroit was facing issues with inconsistent climate conditions across its various production lines, which was affecting both product quality and worker comfort. The existing HVAC system was unable to provide uniform conditions across the sprawling facility.

Solution:

The plant implemented a zoned HVAC system with advanced control technology, allowing for precise temperature and humidity regulation in different areas. The installation included updated insulation and sealing to enhance energy efficiency and system performance.

Results:

The new system improved product quality by maintaining consistent conditions throughout the facility and significantly increased worker comfort. Energy use dropped by 25%, leading to considerable cost savings. The successful upgrade showcased the effectiveness of targeted climate control in optimizing large-scale industrial operations.

Ensuring Compliance in a Pharmaceutical Manufacturing Facility

A major pharmaceutical plant was challenged by stringent regulatory requirements for precise temperature and humidity control in their production and storage areas. The existing HVAC system fell short of meeting these exacting standards.

Solution:

The facility installed a high-precision HVAC system featuring state-of-the-art air filtration, dehumidification, and temperature control. They also integrated a comprehensive monitoring system to provide real-time data and ensure adherence to regulatory requirements.

Results:

The upgraded system guaranteed compliance with industry standards, improved product quality, and reduced contamination risks. Energy efficiency improved by 30%, and the project underscored the importance of precise HVAC technology in maintaining high standards in pharmaceutical manufacturing.

Optimizing Refrigeration Efficiency in a Food Processing Plant

A large food processing facility was experiencing high energy costs and frequent breakdowns in its refrigeration system, crucial for preserving perishable goods. The outdated equipment was unable to keep up with growing demands.

Solution:

The plant implemented a new refrigeration system equipped with energy-efficient compressors and variable-speed fans, along with advanced refrigerant management technologies. The project also involved improving insulation and integrating a smart control system.

Results:

The modernized refrigeration system resulted in a 35% reduction in energy consumption and lower maintenance costs. The facility successfully met increased production demands while maintaining high standards of product quality. The project demonstrated the benefits of advanced HVAC solutions in enhancing efficiency in the food processing sector.

Enhancing Ventilation for Safety in a Chemical Plant

A chemical plant was struggling with inadequate ventilation, leading to poor air quality and potential safety hazards. Compliance with environmental regulations was also a pressing concern due to the outdated ventilation system.

Solution:

The plant upgraded to a high-capacity ventilation system featuring advanced air filtration and exhaust technologies. The new setup included real-time monitoring and control systems to maintain optimal air quality and ensure regulatory compliance.

Results:

The upgraded ventilation system improved air quality, enhanced worker safety, and achieved compliance with environmental standards. Energy costs related to ventilation were reduced by 50%, and working conditions were significantly improved. The successful project highlighted the critical role of modern HVAC technology in meeting safety and regulatory requirements in the chemical industry.

Book 11:

Smart Home Integration with HVAC

Chapter 45: Overview of Smart Home Systems

Definition of Smart Home Systems

Smart home systems are a network of interconnected devices and appliances designed to enhance the functionality, security, and efficiency of residential spaces. These systems utilize the Internet of Things (IoT) technology to allow homeowners to control and automate various aspects of their home environment remotely. By connecting devices through a central hub or smartphone application, users can monitor and manage their home systems with ease, creating a more convenient and efficient living space.

The concept of a smart home encompasses a wide array of devices, including lighting systems, security cameras, smart locks, and HVAC systems. The primary objective is to provide users with greater control over their environment, allowing for personalized experiences that adapt to individual lifestyles. For instance, a smart home system might automatically adjust lighting based on the time of day, lock doors when residents leave, or adjust the thermostat to optimize energy use when the house is unoccupied.

Key Features and Benefits

Smart home systems are equipped with several key features that provide substantial benefits to homeowners:

1. Remote Control: Homeowners can manage their devices from anywhere, using smartphones, tablets, or voice commands. This flexibility allows for adjustments to be made onthefly, whether at home or away.

2. Automation: Many smart home systems offer automation capabilities, enabling devices to operate based on predetermined schedules or triggers. For example, a smart thermostat can lower the temperature at night and raise it before waking up.

3. Energy Efficiency: By optimizing the operation of devices, smart home systems can significantly reduce energy consumption. For instance, smart thermostats can adjust settings based on occupancy, preventing unnecessary heating or cooling.

4. Enhanced Security: Smart home technology enhances security through connected cameras, motion detectors, and alarms. Homeowners can receive realtime alerts about unusual activity and monitor their properties remotely.

5. Improved Comfort: By personalizing environmental settings, smart home systems enhance comfort levels. Homeowners can easily adjust lighting, temperature, and other settings to suit their preferences. Overall, the integration of smart home technology simplifies daily routines, promotes energy savings, and enhances security, making it an attractive option for modern homeowners.

Compatibility with HVAC

How HVAC Systems Can Integrate with Smart Home Technology

The integration of HVAC systems with smart home technology represents a significant advancement in how indoor environments are managed. Smart HVAC solutions allow homeowners to monitor and control their heating and cooling systems remotely, providing greater flexibility and efficiency.

Smart thermostats are a prime example of this integration. These devices connect to the home WiFi network, enabling users to adjust settings through mobile apps. Additionally, many smart thermostats learn from users' behaviors and preferences, optimizing temperature settings automatically. For example, if a homeowner consistently adjusts the temperature down in the evenings, a smart thermostat can learn this behavior and make the adjustment automatically over time.

Moreover, smart sensors can be added to HVAC systems to monitor conditions such as temperature, humidity, and air quality. These sensors provide realtime data that can be used to make informed adjustments to HVAC operations, enhancing comfort and efficiency. For instance, if humidity levels rise, a smart HVAC system can activate dehumidification to maintain a comfortable indoor climate.

The compatibility between HVAC systems and smart home technologies extends to the ability to create zoning systems. Zoning allows for different areas of a home to be heated or cooled independently based on occupancy and preferences. Smart devices can control these zones effectively, ensuring that energy is used efficiently and that comfort is maximized throughout the home.

Overview of Communication Protocols

For smart HVAC systems to communicate effectively with other smart home devices, they rely on various communication protocols. Understanding these protocols is essential for homeowners and professionals looking to implement smart technologies in their HVAC systems.

1. Zigbee: Zigbee is a lowpower, wireless communication protocol designed specifically for shortrange applications. It is widely used in smart home devices due to its ability to form mesh networks, allowing devices to communicate with one another even if they are not directly connected to a central hub. Zigbee is ideal for energyefficient applications, making it suitable for HVAC integrations that require low power consumption.

2. ZWave: Like Zigbee, ZWave is another wireless protocol used in home automation. Operating on a lower frequency than WiFi, ZWave minimizes interference from other wireless networks, providing a reliable connection for smart devices. It also supports mesh networking, enabling devices to communicate over greater distances. ZWave is commonly found in smart thermostats and HVAC controls, allowing seamless integration with other smart home devices.

3. WiFi: WiFi is perhaps the most familiar communication protocol, as it connects devices to the internet and allows for highspeed data transmission. Many smart HVAC devices use WiFi for direct access to the internet, enabling remote control via smartphone apps. While WiFi provides a robust connection, it may consume more power than Zigbee or ZWave, which could be a consideration for devices operating continuously.

In conclusion, the integration of smart home systems with HVAC technology offers homeowners enhanced control, convenience, and energy efficiency. By understanding how these systems work together and the communication protocols that enable them, individuals can make informed decisions about upgrading their HVAC systems to create a smarter, more responsive home environment. As we continue exploring the intersection of smart technology and HVAC, we will delve into specific applications and innovations that are shaping the future of home climate control.

Chapter 46: Popular Smart Thermostats

Google Nest

Features and Installation Process

The Google Nest thermostat is widely recognized for its sleek design and advanced features. It learns your schedule and preferences over time, automatically adjusting temperatures to optimize comfort and energy savings. One of its standout features is the AutoSchedule function, which adapts to your habits and adjusts the temperature accordingly. Additionally, the Nest thermostat can be controlled remotely via the Nest app, allowing users to make adjustments from anywhere.

Installing the Google Nest thermostat is a straightforward process. It typically involves:

- Turn Off Power: Before starting, ensure that power to the HVAC system is turned off to prevent any electrical mishaps.
- Remove the Old Thermostat: Carefully detach the existing thermostat from the wall, taking note of the wiring configuration.
- Connect the Wires: Follow the colorcoded wiring system to connect the wires to the corresponding terminals on the Nest base. The app provides clear guidance during this step.
- Mount the Base: Attach the Nest base to the wall using screws, ensuring it is level.
- Attach the Display: Snap the display onto the base and restore power to the system.

User Interface and EnergySaving Settings

The user interface of the Google Nest is intuitive and visually appealing. It features a highresolution display that shows the current temperature, schedule, and weather updates. Users can easily navigate through settings using the rotating dial or the touchsensitive display.

Nest also offers various energysaving settings, including:

- Eco Temperature: Automatically adjusts the temperature when you're away to conserve energy.
- Home/Away Assist: Uses motion sensors and your phone's location to determine if anyone is home, adjusting temperatures accordingly.
- Energy History: Provides insights into energy usage patterns, helping users make informed decisions about their heating and cooling habits.

Ecobee

Key Functionalities and Smart Sensors

Ecobee thermostats are known for their versatility and advanced features. One of their key functionalities is the use of smart sensors, which help detect temperature variations in different rooms. This allows the system to adjust temperatures based on occupancy and comfort levels in specific areas, ensuring a consistent environment throughout the home.

Ecobee also offers a feature called Home IQ, which provides data on energy usage and savings over time. This data empowers homeowners to make better decisions regarding their heating and cooling habits.

Integration with Other Smart Home Devices

Ecobee thermostats seamlessly integrate with various smart home devices, including Amazon Alexa, Google Assistant, and Apple HomeKit. This compatibility enables voice control and integration with home automation systems, allowing users to create customized routines. For instance, homeowners can program their thermostats to adjust when they arrive home or go to bed, enhancing overall energy efficiency and comfort.

Honeywell Smart Thermostats

Overview of Models and Their Capabilities

Honeywell offers a range of smart thermostats, each designed to meet different user needs. The Honeywell Home T9 is notable for its adaptive temperature control and the ability to work with remote sensors, allowing for zoned heating and cooling. The Honeywell Home RTH9585WF is another popular model, featuring a color touchscreen display and WiFi connectivity.

Each model is equipped with userfriendly interfaces and supports features like scheduling, geofencing, and energy usage reports. Honeywell thermostats also have a robust mobile app that allows for remote control and monitoring.

Comparative Analysis with Other Brands

When comparing Honeywell thermostats with competitors like Google Nest and Ecobee, several distinctions arise. While Google Nest excels in learning capabilities and intuitive design, Honeywell provides more straightforward setups and broader compatibility with older HVAC systems. Ecobee stands out with its smart sensor technology, which can be a deciding factor for homeowners needing precise temperature control in multiple rooms. Ultimately, the choice depends on individual preferences, specific needs, and how well each thermostat fits into the existing home automation ecosystem.

Installation and Setup

StepbyStep Guide for Installation

Installing a smart thermostat can vary slightly between models, but the general process remains consistent:

1. Power Down Your HVAC System: Before beginning, turn off the power to your heating and cooling system to avoid any electrical hazards.
2. Remove the Existing Thermostat: Carefully take off the old thermostat, ensuring to label the wires for easy identification later.
3. Connect the New Thermostat: Use the provided wiring diagram to connect the wires to the appropriate terminals on the smart thermostat.
4. Mount the Thermostat: Secure the thermostat to the wall using screws, ensuring it is mounted level.
5. Power On and Configure: Restore power to your HVAC system and follow the setup instructions provided by the thermostat's app to configure settings.

Troubleshooting Common Installation Issues

While installing a smart thermostat is generally straightforward, homeowners may encounter a few common issues:

- Wiring Conflicts: Ensure that wires are correctly connected to the appropriate terminals. Refer to the thermostat's installation guide if there is any confusion.
- Power Issues: If the thermostat fails to power on, doublecheck that the HVAC system is powered up and that the circuit breaker hasn't tripped.
- WiFi Connectivity: If the thermostat isn't connecting to WiFi, ensure you are within range of the router and that you have entered the correct password. Restarting the router can also resolve connectivity problems.

In summary, this chapter has provided a comprehensive overview of popular smart thermostats, including Google Nest, Ecobee, and Honeywell models. By understanding their features, installation processes, and integration with other smart home devices, homeowners can make informed decisions that enhance their HVAC systems' efficiency and comfort. As we move forward in this book, we will continue exploring how smart technology is revolutionizing HVAC management and improving the overall home environment.

Chapter 47: Voice Control Integration

Overview of Voice Control Systems
Introduction to Amazon Alexa, Google Assistant, and Apple HomeKit

Voice control systems have revolutionized how we interact with technology, offering a handsfree, intuitive way to manage smart home devices. Among the most popular voice control platforms are Amazon Alexa, Google Assistant, and Apple HomeKit. Each of these systems allows users to control their smart devices—including HVAC systems—through simple voice commands, enhancing convenience and usability.

Amazon Alexa is part of the Echo smart speaker line and supports a wide range of smart home devices, including those from various manufacturers. With Alexa, users can ask questions, set reminders, and control their environment using natural language. For example, saying, "Alexa, set the living room temperature to 72 degrees," provides an effortless way to adjust the HVAC system.

Google Assistant, found in Google Home devices, operates similarly. It provides a conversational interface for managing devices, performing searches, and controlling smart home functions. Users can say, "Hey Google, increase the temperature by two degrees," to achieve instant control over their HVAC settings.

Apple HomeKit offers an integrated smart home experience for iOS users. It allows for seamless control of compatible devices using Siri, Apple's virtual assistant. Users can issue commands such as, "Siri, turn off the heat in the bedroom," to manage their HVAC systems effectively.

These voice control systems enhance the smart home experience by allowing homeowners to interact with their devices in a more natural and accessible manner.

Connecting HVAC Systems to Voice Assistants
StepbyStep Instructions for Setup and Configuration

Integrating your HVAC system with voice control systems can be a straightforward process. While the specific steps may vary depending on the smart thermostat or HVAC device, the general setup process involves:

1. Ensure Compatibility: Check that your HVAC system or smart thermostat is compatible with your chosen voice assistant (Alexa, Google Assistant, or HomeKit).

2. Install the Smart Thermostat: Follow the installation instructions for your smart thermostat as outlined in previous chapters. Ensure that the thermostat is connected to your home WiFi network.

3. Download the App: Install the relevant app for your voice assistant (Amazon Alexa app, Google Home app, or Apple Home app) on your smartphone.

4. Add the Device:

For Amazon Alexa: Open the Alexa app, tap on "Devices," then "+" to add a new device. Select your thermostat brand and follow the onscreen prompts to link the accounts.

For Google Assistant: Open the Google Home app, tap "+," select "Set up device," then "Works with Google." Find your thermostat's brand and follow the prompts to connect.

For Apple HomeKit: Open the Home app, tap the "+" icon, select "Add Accessory," and use your camera to scan the HomeKit setup code found on your thermostat.

5. Complete the Setup: Once your device is added, configure any specific settings within the app, such as room assignments or preferences for temperature ranges.

Creating Voice Commands for Temperature Control and Scheduling

Once your HVAC system is connected to your voice assistant, creating voice commands becomes a simple task. The systems generally understand natural language, making it easy to issue commands related to temperature control and scheduling. Here are some examples:

Temperature Control:
- ✓ "Alexa, set the thermostat to 75 degrees."
- ✓ "Hey Google, turn up the heat in the living room."
- ✓ "Siri, adjust the temperature to 68 degrees."

Scheduling:
- ✓ "Alexa, schedule the thermostat to lower the temperature at 10 PM."
- ✓ "Hey Google, set a routine to cool down the house at 4 PM every day."
- ✓ "Siri, turn off the heating at 11 PM."

These commands enable users to manage their HVAC systems efficiently without having to physically interact with the thermostat.

Customizing Voice Commands

Tips for Optimizing Voice Interactions with HVAC Systems

To enhance the experience of using voice control for HVAC management, consider the following tips:

- Use Specific Names: Assign specific names to rooms and devices in your smart home app to avoid confusion. For example, naming the thermostat in the master bedroom "Master Bedroom Thermostat" allows for clear commands.

- Keep Commands Simple: Use straightforward language when issuing commands. Phrasing such as "Set living room temperature to 70" is more effective than more complex sentences.

- Create Routines: Utilize the routine features in your voice assistant's app. Routines allow multiple commands to be triggered with a single phrase. For example, saying "Good night" could set the thermostat to a specific temperature, turn off lights, and lock doors.

Examples of Practical Voice Commands

Here are some practical voice commands that homeowners can use to interact with their HVAC systems effectively:

- ✓ "Alexa, what's the temperature in the house?"
- ✓ "Google, lower the thermostat by 3 degrees."
- ✓ "Siri, turn off the air conditioning."
- ✓ "Alexa, set the HVAC to eco mode."
- ✓ "Google, start cooling the house at 5 PM."

These commands not only streamline the user experience but also enhance the overall efficiency of the HVAC system by allowing users to maintain control over their indoor environment effortlessly. In summary, voice control integration is a gamechanger for smart HVAC management, allowing for seamless interaction between homeowners and their heating and cooling systems. With the ability to control and automate HVAC functions through natural language commands, users can enjoy greater convenience, improved energy efficiency, and enhanced comfort in their living spaces. As we proceed in this book, we will delve into more aspects of smart home technology and how it can further optimize HVAC performance and user experience.

Chapter 48: Thermal Energy Storage in Smart HVAC Systems

Overview of Thermal Energy Storage (TES)

Thermal Energy Storage (TES) is an innovative technology that allows HVAC systems to store thermal energy for later use. By shifting energy consumption to off-peak hours, TES systems help reduce overall energy costs, enhance grid stability, and promote the use of renewable energy sources. This chapter explores the principles of thermal energy storage, its applications in smart HVAC systems, and its benefits for energy efficiency and sustainability.

Types of Thermal Energy Storage

Ice Storage Systems:

Ice storage systems create ice during off-peak hours (typically at night) when electricity rates are lower. This ice is then used to cool the building during peak demand periods by circulating chilled water through the HVAC system. Ice storage is particularly effective in commercial buildings with high cooling loads, allowing significant reductions in energy costs.

Chilled Water Storage:

Similar to ice storage, chilled water storage systems chill water during off-peak hours. This chilled water is then stored in insulated tanks and used for cooling during peak hours. This approach provides flexibility and efficiency, especially for large commercial and industrial applications.

Phase Change Materials (PCMs):

PCMs absorb and release thermal energy as they change states (e.g., from solid to liquid). These materials can be integrated into building materials or used in dedicated storage systems. By using PCMs, buildings can effectively manage temperature fluctuations, providing stable indoor climates while reducing the load on HVAC systems.

Benefits of Thermal Energy Storage

Cost Savings:

By shifting energy consumption to off-peak periods, TES systems take advantage of lower electricity rates, resulting in significant cost savings. This is especially beneficial for commercial buildings that face high demand charges during peak usage times.

Peak Load Management:

TES helps alleviate stress on the electrical grid during peak demand periods. By reducing the need for additional energy generation during these times, TES contributes to a more reliable and stable energy infrastructure.

Integration with Renewables:

Thermal energy storage systems can be paired with renewable energy sources, such as solar or wind. For example, excess solar energy can be used to produce ice or chilled water during the day, which can then be utilized for cooling in the evening. This integration enhances the overall sustainability of the energy system.

Applications in Smart HVAC Systems

Smart HVAC systems that incorporate thermal energy storage provide enhanced capabilities for energy management and optimization. These systems can leverage advanced algorithms and real-time data to determine the optimal times for energy storage and usage.

- **Demand Response Capabilities:**
  By integrating TES with smart HVAC systems, buildings can participate in demand response programs. During peak demand periods, the system can automatically adjust cooling loads by utilizing stored energy instead of drawing from the grid, reducing costs and contributing to grid stability.
- **User-Centric Control:**
  Smart thermostats and building management systems can monitor occupancy patterns, weather forecasts, and energy prices to optimize the charging and discharging of thermal storage. This ensures maximum comfort for occupants while minimizing energy costs.

Case Study: Implementing TES in a Commercial Building

Background:
A large commercial office building in a metropolitan area faced high energy costs due to peak cooling demands during summer months. The building management team sought to implement a solution that would reduce energy expenses and enhance sustainability.

Implementation:
The team installed an ice storage system that produced ice overnight using off-peak electricity. The system was integrated with the building's existing smart HVAC controls, allowing for automated operation based on occupancy and energy pricing.

Results:
Following the implementation of the ice storage system, the building reported a 35% reduction in cooling costs. The ability to shift energy use to off-peak hours significantly decreased demand charges. Additionally, the system enhanced occupant comfort by maintaining stable indoor temperatures, even during peak heat events.

Future Trends in Thermal Energy Storage

The future of thermal energy storage in HVAC systems looks promising, with several emerging trends:

- **Advanced Materials:** Research into new phase change materials and storage solutions continues to enhance the efficiency and effectiveness of TES systems, making them more viable for a broader range of applications.

- **Smart Integration:** As smart building technologies evolve, the integration of TES with other building systems (lighting, energy management) will provide comprehensive solutions for energy efficiency and sustainability.
- **Regulatory Support:** As governments and utilities promote energy efficiency and renewable energy adoption, regulatory frameworks may increasingly support the deployment of thermal energy storage technologies.

Thermal energy storage represents a significant advancement in the quest for energy efficiency within HVAC systems. By enabling the storage of thermal energy for later use, these systems can effectively reduce costs, alleviate peak demand pressures, and integrate seamlessly with renewable energy sources. As smart technologies continue to evolve, the role of thermal energy storage in optimizing HVAC performance will undoubtedly grow, contributing to a more sustainable and energy-efficient future.

Chapter 49: Troubleshooting Smart HVAC Systems

Common Issues with Smart Integration
Overview of Potential Problems and Their Causes

As homeowners increasingly adopt smart HVAC systems, they may encounter a variety of integration challenges. Understanding these common issues is crucial for maintaining optimal performance and comfort. Some potential problems include:

1. Connectivity Issues: Smart thermostats and devices rely on stable WiFi connections to function effectively. Common causes of connectivity issues include weak WiFi signals, network interruptions, or conflicts with other connected devices.
2. Compatibility Problems: Not all smart HVAC devices are compatible with every system. Issues may arise when trying to integrate devices from different manufacturers, especially if they use different communication protocols (e.g., Zigbee, ZWave, WiFi).
3. Software Bugs: Like any technology, smart devices can experience software bugs or glitches. These issues may prevent devices from responding correctly to commands or lead to erratic performance.
4. Power Supply Issues: Smart thermostats and sensors require a consistent power supply. Problems can arise from low battery levels or wiring issues that prevent devices from functioning correctly.
5. Sensor Malfunctions: Smart sensors that monitor temperature, humidity, or occupancy may sometimes provide inaccurate readings due to obstructions, dirt, or incorrect calibration.

By recognizing these potential issues, homeowners can take proactive measures to troubleshoot and resolve problems as they arise.

Step-by-Step Troubleshooting Guide
Identifying and Resolving Connectivity Issues

Connectivity problems are among the most common issues faced by smart HVAC users. Here's a stepbystep guide to diagnosing and fixing these problems:

1. Check WiFi Connection: Ensure that your WiFi network is operational. You can do this by testing other devices connected to the same network.
2. Reboot the Router: Sometimes, simply rebooting the router can resolve connectivity issues. Unplug the router, wait for 30 seconds, and then plug it back in.
3. Device Proximity: Make sure that the smart thermostat or device is within range of the WiFi signal. If it's too far from the router, consider moving the router or using WiFi extenders.

4. Network Conflicts: Ensure that there are no IP address conflicts on the network. Restart the smart device to refresh its connection.

5. Firmware Updates: Check for any available firmware updates for the smart device. Manufacturers often release updates to fix bugs and improve connectivity.

6. Reconfigure the Device: If the issue persists, remove the device from the smart home app and readd it, following the setup instructions carefully.

Addressing Performance Problems with Smart Devices

When smart HVAC devices are not performing as expected, follow these steps:

1. Reset the Device: Many smart devices have a reset option. Consult the user manual for instructions on how to reset the device to its factory settings.

2. Check for Obstructions: Ensure that sensors are not obstructed by furniture, curtains, or other objects that may affect their ability to monitor conditions accurately.

3. Calibration: If the device is providing incorrect readings, recalibrate it according to the manufacturer's instructions. This may involve adjusting settings in the app.

4. Inspect Wiring: For hardwired devices, check that all connections are secure and that there are no damaged wires. If you notice any issues, consult a professional.

5. Test the HVAC System: If the smart device controls the HVAC system, ensure that the system is functioning correctly. Manually adjust the system to see if it responds to direct commands.

6. Review Settings: Doublecheck settings within the smart home app. Sometimes, settings may have been unintentionally changed, affecting performance.

When to Seek Professional Help

Signs That Indicate the Need for Expert Assistance

While many smart HVAC issues can be resolved through troubleshooting, there are times when professional assistance is necessary. Here are some signs that it may be time to call in an expert:

1. Persistent Connectivity Issues: If connectivity problems persist after following troubleshooting steps, there may be underlying network issues or device malfunctions that require professional assessment.

2. System Performance Decline: If the HVAC system is not responding to the smart thermostat or devices, or if there are drastic changes in temperature regulation, this could indicate a more serious issue with the HVAC system itself.

3. Complex Integration Challenges: If integrating new smart devices with an existing HVAC system proves overly complicated, a professional can help ensure compatibility and proper setup.

4. Wiring Problems: If you suspect wiring issues or if the installation requires significant electrical work, it's best to consult a licensed HVAC technician to avoid safety hazards.

Resources for Finding HVAC Professionals Familiar with Smart Technology

Finding the right professional to assist with smart HVAC systems is essential. Here are some resources to help:

1. Professional Organizations: Associations such as the Air Conditioning Contractors of America (ACCA) and the American Society of Heating, Refrigerating and AirConditioning Engineers (ASHRAE) offer directories of certified professionals.
2. Local HVAC Companies: Many HVAC service providers now specialize in smart home technology. Look for companies with positive reviews and specific experience with smart systems.
3. Online Platforms: Websites like HomeAdvisor, Angie's List, and Thumbtack allow homeowners to search for and compare HVAC professionals based on expertise and customer feedback.
4. Manufacturer Recommendations: Many smart device manufacturers provide lists of authorized service providers who are familiar with their products. Check the manufacturer's website for more information.

In conclusion, troubleshooting smart HVAC systems requires an understanding of common issues, effective problemsolving techniques, and the knowledge of when to seek professional help. By following the guidelines outlined in this chapter, homeowners can enhance the performance and reliability of their smart HVAC systems, ensuring that their indoor environments remain comfortable and efficient. As we progress further in this book, we will continue to explore the integration of smart technology in HVAC systems and its impact on modern living.

Book 12:

The Role of HVAC in Health and Wellness

Chapter 50: Air Quality and Its Impact on Health

Indoor Air Quality (IAQ) refers to the condition of the air within buildings and its impact on the health and comfort of occupants. It encompasses a variety of factors, including temperature, humidity, ventilation, and the presence of pollutants. IAQ is particularly significant because people spend a substantial amount of their time indoors—often estimated to be as high as 90%. Poor indoor air quality can lead to various health issues and negatively affect overall wellbeing.

The importance of maintaining good IAQ cannot be overstated. Highquality indoor air contributes to enhanced comfort, improved productivity, and better health outcomes. Conversely, compromised IAQ can lead to discomfort, decreased productivity, and increased health risks. It is vital for homeowners, employers, and facility managers to prioritize IAQ to create healthier living and working environments.

Common Pollutants and Their Sources

Numerous pollutants can affect indoor air quality, each originating from different sources. Some of the most common indoor air pollutants include:

Volatile Organic Compounds (VOCs): These are emitted from a variety of household products, including paints, cleaning agents, pesticides, and building materials. VOCs can cause both shortterm and longterm health effects.

Particulate Matter (PM): This includes dust, dirt, and smoke particles that can be inhaled. Sources of PM in indoor environments can include cooking, burning candles, and smoking.

Carbon Monoxide (CO): A colorless, odorless gas produced by incomplete combustion of fuels. Common sources include gas appliances, fireplaces, and vehicle exhaust in attached garages.

Mold and Mildew: These fungi thrive in damp conditions and can produce spores that negatively impact air quality. High humidity levels and water leaks can promote mold growth.

Allergens: Common indoor allergens include pet dander, dust mites, and pollen. These can exacerbate respiratory conditions such as asthma and allergies.

Identifying these pollutants and their sources is the first step in addressing and improving indoor air quality.

Health Effects of Poor IAQ

Overview of Respiratory Issues and Allergies

Poor indoor air quality is directly linked to a range of respiratory issues and allergies. Common health problems associated with poor IAQ include:

Asthma: Exposure to indoor pollutants can trigger asthma attacks in sensitive individuals. Dust mites, mold, and pet dander are known allergens that can exacerbate this condition.

Allergic Rhinitis: Also known as hay fever, allergic rhinitis can be triggered by indoor allergens such as pollen, dust mites, and mold spores. Symptoms include sneezing, runny nose, and itchy eyes.

Chronic Obstructive Pulmonary Disease (COPD): Longterm exposure to indoor air pollutants can contribute to the development of COPD, a group of lung diseases that block airflow and make breathing difficult.

Long-Term Health Impacts

In addition to immediate health effects, poor indoor air quality can lead to longterm health problems. Research has shown that chronic exposure to indoor pollutants can increase the risk of developing serious health conditions, including:

Lung Cancer: Prolonged exposure to certain carcinogens, such as formaldehyde and benzene, found in indoor environments can increase the risk of lung cancer.

Cardiovascular Disease: Studies have linked poor IAQ to an increased risk of heart disease. Pollutants such as particulate matter can enter the bloodstream and contribute to cardiovascular problems.

Neurological Issues: Emerging research suggests that exposure to indoor pollutants may impact cognitive function and mental health, potentially leading to conditions like depression and anxiety.

Understanding these health implications highlights the critical need for effective indoor air quality management.

In summary, indoor air quality plays a crucial role in overall health and wellbeing. By understanding the common pollutants, their sources, and the health impacts of poor IAQ, individuals can take proactive steps to improve their indoor environments. HVAC systems are essential tools in this effort, providing filtration, ventilation, and humidity control that contribute to healthier living spaces. As we continue to explore the role of HVAC in health and wellness, we will examine additional factors and strategies that further enhance the quality of indoor environments.

Chapter 51: HVAC Systems and Sleep Quality

Temperature and Sleep

Research on Optimal Sleeping Temperatures

Numerous studies have explored the relationship between temperature and sleep quality, revealing that maintaining an optimal sleeping temperature is crucial for restful sleep. Research indicates that the ideal temperature range for sleep typically falls between 60°F and 67°F (15°C to 19°C). Within this range, the body's core temperature can decrease naturally, facilitating the onset of sleep.

A study published in the Journal of Clinical Sleep Medicine highlights that individuals who sleep in cooler environments report better sleep quality and experience fewer awakenings during the night. Conversely, higher temperatures can disrupt sleep patterns, leading to increased restlessness and a greater likelihood of waking up throughout the night. This underscores the importance of regulating bedroom temperatures as part of a holistic approach to improving sleep quality.

Effects of Temperature Fluctuations on Sleep Quality

Temperature fluctuations during the night can significantly impact sleep quality. If the bedroom is too warm or too cold, it can lead to discomfort, making it difficult for individuals to fall asleep or stay asleep. Nighttime awakenings can be exacerbated by sudden changes in temperature, disrupting the sleep cycle and reducing the overall quality of rest.

For instance, a warm room can lead to increased sweating, restlessness, and difficulty in achieving deeper sleep stages, such as REM (Rapid Eye Movement) sleep, which is essential for cognitive functioning and emotional regulation. On the other hand, excessively cold temperatures may cause individuals to wake frequently to adjust blankets or reposition themselves for comfort.

To mitigate these effects, maintaining a stable temperature throughout the night is critical. HVAC systems that allow for precise temperature control can help achieve this stability, ensuring that the sleeping environment remains conducive to restful sleep.

Air Circulation and Comfort

Importance of Proper Airflow in Bedrooms

Proper airflow is another crucial element in creating an ideal sleep environment. Stagnant air can lead to discomfort, making it challenging to achieve restful sleep. Inadequate air circulation may also contribute to the buildup of humidity, allergens, and indoor pollutants, which can negatively affect sleep quality.

Good air circulation helps maintain a consistent temperature and humidity level, promoting a comfortable environment conducive to sleep. Additionally, circulating fresh air can enhance indoor air quality, reducing the presence of allergens such as dust mites and pet dander, which may trigger respiratory issues and disrupt sleep.

Strategies for Achieving Ideal Sleep Conditions

To optimize airflow and comfort in the bedroom, consider implementing the following strategies:

1. Adjust HVAC Vents: Ensure that HVAC vents are positioned correctly to promote airflow throughout the room. Avoid blocking vents with furniture or curtains, as this can hinder airflow.
2. Use Ceiling Fans: Ceiling fans can help circulate air, providing a gentle breeze that enhances comfort while allowing the thermostat to be set at a slightly higher temperature without sacrificing sleep quality.
3. Implement Zoning Systems: If the HVAC system allows for zoning, configure it to provide tailored heating or cooling to the bedroom while ensuring that airflow is optimized for sleep.
4. Open Windows (When Possible): Fresh outdoor air can improve indoor air quality and circulation. However, this should be done cautiously, as outdoor temperature and air quality should be considered.
5. Regular Maintenance: Ensure that the HVAC system is regularly serviced to maintain optimal performance. This includes cleaning or replacing filters, which can improve airflow and enhance air quality.

Smart Technologies for Sleep Improvement

Using Smart Thermostats for Personalized Sleep Settings

Smart thermostats offer advanced features that can significantly enhance sleep quality by allowing for personalized temperature settings tailored to individual preferences. These devices can learn users' schedules and adjust temperatures accordingly. For instance, a smart thermostat can automatically lower the temperature before bedtime and then gradually increase it in the morning to create a comfortable wakeup environment.

Many smart thermostats also include scheduling features, allowing users to set specific temperature preferences for different times of the day. By automating temperature adjustments, smart thermostats help maintain an optimal sleep environment without the need for manual intervention.

Integrating HVAC with Sleep Monitoring Devices

The integration of HVAC systems with sleep monitoring devices represents a cuttingedge approach to enhancing sleep quality. Sleep trackers, such as wearable devices or smart mattresses, provide data on sleep patterns, duration, and disturbances. This information can be used to adjust the HVAC system dynamically.

For example, if a sleep monitor detects that a person is restless due to high temperatures, it can communicate with the smart thermostat to lower the temperature, creating a more conducive environment for sleep. This integration not only optimizes comfort but also allows for datadriven insights that can help individuals improve their overall sleep quality.

In conclusion, the relationship between HVAC systems and sleep quality is significant, with temperature regulation, airflow, and innovative technologies playing essential roles. By understanding the optimal conditions for sleep and leveraging smart HVAC solutions, individuals can create an environment that promotes restful and restorative sleep. As we continue through this book, we will explore further how HVAC systems can contribute to health and wellness in various aspects of our daily lives.

Chapter 52: Reducing Virus Spread with HVAC

HVAC Filtration Systems
Overview of Filtration Technologies (HEPA, MERV Ratings)

HVAC filtration systems are critical components in maintaining indoor air quality, particularly in reducing the transmission of airborne viruses. Various filtration technologies are designed to capture particulate matter, including viruses, bacteria, dust, and allergens. Two commonly referenced systems are HEPA (HighEfficiency Particulate Air) filters and MERV (Minimum Efficiency Reporting Value) ratings.

HEPA Filters

HEPA filters are highly efficient in trapping small particles, including those as tiny as 0.3 microns with an efficiency of 99.97%. This capability makes HEPA filters particularly effective at capturing airborne viruses and bacteria. These filters are widely used in hospitals, laboratories, and homes, particularly in areas where maintaining high air quality is crucial. When installed in HVAC systems, HEPA filters can significantly reduce the concentration of airborne pathogens, providing an added layer of protection for occupants.

MERV Ratings

MERV ratings range from 1 to 16, with higher ratings indicating a filter's ability to capture smaller particles. Filters with a MERV rating of 13 or higher are recommended for effectively reducing airborne viruses and other pathogens. Understanding MERV ratings helps homeowners and facility managers select appropriate filters based on their specific needs and the level of air quality they wish to achieve.

Importance of Regular Filter Replacement and Maintenance

Maintaining HVAC filtration systems requires regular inspection and replacement of filters to ensure optimal performance. Over time, filters can become clogged with dust and particles, reducing their efficiency and airflow. Regular replacement—typically every 1 to 3 months, depending on usage and filter type—ensures that the system operates effectively and continues to capture harmful particles.

In addition to replacing filters, routine maintenance of the HVAC system, including cleaning the ductwork and checking for leaks, is essential. Proper maintenance not only enhances the system's ability to filter air but also improves overall energy efficiency and prolongs the lifespan of the equipment.

Ventilation Strategies to Minimize Transmission
How Increased Ventilation Can Reduce Airborne Illnesses

Increasing ventilation is one of the most effective strategies for minimizing the spread of airborne illnesses within indoor environments. Enhanced ventilation helps dilute and remove contaminants, including viruses, from the air, reducing the risk of transmission among occupants.

Research indicates that wellventilated spaces can significantly lower the concentration of airborne pathogens. By increasing the rate of fresh air exchange, HVAC systems can help create healthier environments, particularly in hightraffic areas like schools, offices, and public spaces. Strategies for increasing ventilation include using outdoor air intake, exhaust fans, and opening windows when weather permits.

Recommendations for Effective Ventilation in Various Settings

Different environments may require tailored ventilation strategies. Here are some recommendations for effective ventilation in various settings:

1. Residential Settings: Encourage the use of exhaust fans in kitchens and bathrooms to remove contaminants. Consider integrating a wholehouse ventilation system that allows for the introduction of fresh outdoor air while managing humidity levels.
2. Commercial Spaces: Implement demandcontrolled ventilation (DCV) systems that adjust airflow based on occupancy levels. Use CO2 sensors to monitor air quality and adjust ventilation rates accordingly.
3. Educational Facilities: Increase outdoor air ventilation rates in classrooms and common areas to promote healthy air circulation. Implement a schedule for regular airing out of spaces when they are unoccupied.
4. Healthcare Settings: Ensure that HVAC systems in healthcare facilities meet or exceed guidelines for ventilation rates as outlined by organizations such as the Centers for Disease Control and Prevention (CDC). Use specialized air filtration systems in areas where infection control is critical.

By tailoring ventilation strategies to the specific needs of different settings, the risk of airborne illnesses can be significantly reduced.

Case Studies

Examples of HVAC Systems Successfully Reducing Virus Transmission in Public Spaces

Several case studies illustrate the effectiveness of HVAC systems in mitigating the spread of viruses in public spaces:

1. **Airports:** In a study conducted at a major international airport, the implementation of advanced HVAC systems equipped with HEPA filters and UVC light technology demonstrated a marked

reduction in airborne viral load in terminal areas. The airport's commitment to increasing ventilation rates and using highefficiency filtration systems provided travelers with safer environments.

2. **Schools:** A public school district that upgraded its HVAC systems to include MERV 13 filters and enhanced ventilation protocols reported a decrease in respiratory illnesses among students and staff. The introduction of a monitoring system to track indoor air quality helped maintain optimal conditions and promote health during flu season.

3. **Office Buildings:** A large corporate office implemented a new HVAC strategy that involved increased outdoor air intake and improved filtration. Postimplementation studies showed a significant reduction in sick leave among employees, attributed to enhanced air quality and reduced viral transmission.

These case studies highlight the critical role HVAC systems play in public health, particularly during times of increased concern about airborne diseases. By prioritizing effective filtration, ventilation, and maintenance, facilities can create safer environments that contribute to the overall health and wellbeing of occupants.

In conclusion, HVAC systems are vital in reducing virus transmission and improving indoor air quality. Through effective filtration, increased ventilation, and regular maintenance, these systems can significantly mitigate the risk of airborne illnesses. As we progress in this book, we will explore further aspects of how HVAC technologies contribute to health and wellness in various environments.

Chapter 53: Mental Health and Indoor Comfort

Environmental Comfort and Mental WellBeing
The Connection Between HVAC Comfort and Psychological Health

The environment in which we live significantly impacts our mental health and overall wellbeing. Environmental comfort, primarily influenced by temperature, humidity, and air quality, plays a crucial role in shaping our mood, productivity, and emotional state. Research indicates that optimal indoor climate conditions can lead to improved mental health outcomes, while discomfort can exacerbate stress, anxiety, and feelings of unease.

HVAC systems are pivotal in regulating indoor comfort. They not only maintain a comfortable temperature but also control humidity levels and ensure adequate ventilation. A wellfunctioning HVAC system can create an environment conducive to relaxation, focus, and overall mental clarity. Conversely, an uncomfortable or poorly ventilated space can lead to irritability, distraction, and decreased cognitive performance.

How Temperature and Air Quality Impact Mood and Productivity

Studies have shown that temperature has a direct correlation with mood and productivity. The ideal temperature for comfort and focus typically ranges from 68°F to 72°F (20°C to 22°C). When temperatures rise above or fall below this range, individuals may experience increased discomfort, leading to frustration and decreased motivation. A study published in the journal Building and Environment found that productivity declined significantly when office temperatures exceeded 77°F (25°C), highlighting the importance of temperature regulation for maintaining focus and efficiency in work environments.

Air quality is equally crucial for mental wellbeing. Poor indoor air quality, characterized by high levels of pollutants, allergens, and humidity, can lead to headaches, fatigue, and cognitive decline. Contaminants such as volatile organic compounds (VOCs) and particulate matter can exacerbate symptoms of anxiety and depression. A clean, wellventilated environment contributes to improved cognitive function and emotional stability, enhancing overall mental health.

Creating Comfortable Spaces
Tips for Adjusting HVAC Settings to Enhance Comfort

To foster an environment that promotes mental wellbeing, homeowners and facility managers can take several practical steps to adjust HVAC settings:

1. Optimize Temperature Settings: Regularly monitor and adjust thermostat settings to maintain an ideal temperature range. Consider implementing smart thermostats that learn preferences and adjust settings automatically based on occupancy.

2. Maintain Indoor Air Quality: Invest in highquality air filters and ensure regular replacement. Utilize HEPA filters to capture allergens and pollutants, and consider installing air purifiers to enhance air quality further.

3. Utilize Zoning Systems: If applicable, use zoning systems to tailor heating and cooling to different areas based on occupancy. This approach can help maintain comfort in frequently used spaces while conserving energy in less occupied areas.

4. Control Humidity Levels: Aim for a relative humidity level between 30% and 50%. Use dehumidifiers in damp areas to prevent mold growth and ensure that HVAC systems are equipped to manage humidity effectively.

5. Ventilation: Ensure that the space is adequately ventilated to bring in fresh air and remove stale air. Consider utilizing natural ventilation strategies, such as opening windows when conditions allow, to improve indoor air quality.

The Role of Lighting and Color in Promoting Mental WellBeing

In addition to HVAC settings, the psychological impact of lighting and color in indoor environments should not be overlooked. Natural light has been shown to enhance mood and promote mental health. Whenever possible, design spaces to maximize exposure to natural light.

Lighting: Use adjustable lighting systems that allow for changes in intensity and color temperature. Warmer light tones can create a cozy atmosphere conducive to relaxation, while cooler tones can enhance alertness and focus.

Color Psychology: Colors have psychological effects that can influence mood. Soft blues and greens are often associated with calmness and relaxation, while yellows and oranges can promote energy and creativity. When designing spaces, consider the colors of walls, furniture, and decor to create an environment that aligns with desired emotional outcomes.

Case Studies

RealWorld Examples of How HVAC Improvements Have Positively Impacted Mental Health in Work and Home Environments

Several case studies illustrate the positive impact of HVAC improvements on mental health in various settings:

1. **Corporate Office Revamp:** A technology company recognized the importance of employee wellbeing and undertook a major renovation of its office space. By upgrading the HVAC system to include advanced air filtration and improved temperature control, they created a more comfortable work environment. Employee surveys conducted postrenovation revealed increased job satisfaction and productivity, as workers reported feeling more focused and less fatigued.

2. **Educational Facilities:** A school district implemented a comprehensive HVAC upgrade across several schools, emphasizing enhanced ventilation and air quality. The results were striking: a significant reduction in student absenteeism due to respiratory illnesses, coupled with improved academic performance. Teachers noted that students were more engaged and focused, attributing this change to the healthier classroom environment.

3. **Residential Enhancements:** A family experiencing heightened levels of stress and anxiety attributed their discomfort to poor air quality and fluctuating temperatures in their home. After installing a smart HVAC system with enhanced filtration and better zoning capabilities, they reported substantial improvements in their overall wellbeing. The family experienced better sleep quality, reduced allergy symptoms, and a more harmonious home environment.

These case studies demonstrate the profound effect that welldesigned HVAC systems can have on mental health and overall quality of life. By prioritizing environmental comfort and air quality, individuals and organizations can foster spaces that enhance wellbeing, productivity, and happiness.

In conclusion, the relationship between HVAC systems and mental health is multifaceted, encompassing temperature regulation, air quality management, and thoughtful environmental design. By implementing strategies to optimize indoor comfort, individuals can significantly improve their mental wellbeing. As we continue exploring the role of HVAC in health and wellness, we will delve into further factors and solutions that contribute to creating healthier living and working environments.

Chapter 54: Humidity Control for Wellness

The Role of Humidity in Health
Understanding the Effects of Humidity on Health and Comfort

Humidity, the measure of moisture in the air, plays a crucial role in maintaining a healthy and comfortable indoor environment. It affects not only our physical comfort but also our overall health. The ideal relative humidity level for most indoor environments is typically between 30% and 50%. When humidity levels fall within this range, the air feels comfortable, and the risk of health issues is minimized.

Low humidity can lead to a variety of discomforts and health problems. When indoor air is excessively dry, it can cause dry skin, irritated eyes, and respiratory discomfort. Mucous membranes may dry out, increasing susceptibility to colds, flu, and other infections. Additionally, low humidity can exacerbate conditions like asthma and allergies, as dry air can irritate the airways.

Conversely, high humidity levels can create a breeding ground for mold, dust mites, and other allergens. These can trigger allergic reactions and respiratory issues. High humidity can also make the air feel warmer than it is, leading to discomfort and reduced productivity. The perception of temperature can rise by several degrees when humidity is high, making it essential to manage humidity levels effectively.

Common Issues Related to High or Low Humidity Levels

The effects of humidity on health and comfort are influenced by how it fluctuates. Common issues associated with high humidity include:

Mold Growth: High humidity can lead to the proliferation of mold and mildew, which can negatively impact indoor air quality and pose serious health risks, particularly for individuals with respiratory conditions.

Dust Mites: These microscopic creatures thrive in humid environments. They are a common allergen, and their presence can exacerbate allergies and asthma symptoms.

Discomfort: High humidity can cause a feeling of stickiness, making it difficult to cool down and leading to increased discomfort, particularly in hot weather.

On the other hand, issues related to low humidity include:

Dry Skin and Mucous Membranes: Low humidity can lead to skin irritation, chapped lips, and dry eyes. Respiratory pathways may also become dry and irritated, increasing the risk of infections.

Static Electricity: Dry air increases the occurrence of static electricity, which can be annoying and may damage sensitive electronics.

Worsening of Allergies and Asthma: Low humidity can exacerbate allergies and asthma due to dry air irritating the airways and making breathing uncomfortable.

HVAC Solutions for Humidity Management

Technologies for Controlling Humidity (Dehumidifiers, Humidistats)

HVAC systems can be equipped with various technologies to effectively manage indoor humidity levels:

Dehumidifiers: These devices are specifically designed to remove excess moisture from the air. They are particularly beneficial in regions with high humidity levels or in areas of the home prone to moisture accumulation, such as basements and bathrooms. Dehumidifiers work by drawing in humid air, cooling it to condense moisture, and then expelling drier air back into the room.

Humidistats: These devices measure the relative humidity in the air and help regulate the operation of HVAC systems to maintain optimal humidity levels. A humidistat can automatically activate dehumidifiers or adjust HVAC settings based on current humidity levels, ensuring a balanced environment.

Integrated HVAC Systems: Many modern HVAC systems come equipped with builtin humidity control features. These systems can monitor and adjust both temperature and humidity levels simultaneously, providing comprehensive climate control.

Best Practices for Maintaining Balanced Humidity Levels in Homes and Workplaces

To achieve optimal humidity levels, homeowners and facility managers can adopt the following best practices:

1. Regular Maintenance: Ensure that HVAC systems are regularly serviced to maintain efficiency. This includes checking and cleaning air filters, inspecting ductwork, and calibrating humidistats.

2. Monitor Humidity Levels: Use hygrometers to measure indoor humidity and monitor fluctuations. This information can help inform decisions about necessary adjustments.

3. Ventilation: Promote proper ventilation throughout the space. Use exhaust fans in bathrooms and kitchens to remove excess moisture, especially during activities like showering or cooking.

4. Seal Leaks: Inspect the building for leaks that may allow moisture from outside to enter. Seal gaps around windows, doors, and ducts to prevent excess moisture infiltration.

5. Adjust Thermostat Settings: In humid conditions, consider using air conditioning to help reduce indoor humidity. Air conditioning systems naturally dehumidify the air as they cool it.

6. Use Dehumidifiers When Necessary: In particularly humid climates or in spaces where humidity tends to accumulate, consider using standalone dehumidifiers to maintain comfort.

LongTerm Health Benefits

The Impact of Proper Humidity Control on Respiratory Health and Comfort

Maintaining balanced humidity levels can yield significant longterm health benefits. Proper humidity control plays a vital role in supporting respiratory health by preventing conditions that could exacerbate asthma, allergies, and other respiratory issues. Studies have shown that individuals living in environments with controlled humidity levels experience fewer respiratory infections and allergyrelated symptoms.

Additionally, maintaining optimal humidity contributes to overall comfort and wellbeing. A wellbalanced indoor environment can lead to improved sleep quality, increased productivity, and enhanced mood. By reducing discomfort and the prevalence of allergens and irritants, individuals are likely to experience better physical and mental health.

Recommendations for Homeowners and Businesses to Monitor and Adjust Humidity Levels

To ensure effective humidity control, homeowners and businesses should consider the following recommendations:

1. Install Humidity Sensors: Incorporate humidity sensors into HVAC systems or use standalone hygrometers to monitor humidity levels continuously.

2. Educate Occupants: Raise awareness about the importance of humidity control among family members or employees. Encourage practices that contribute to maintaining balanced humidity levels, such as using exhaust fans and closing doors during humid conditions.

3. Create a Maintenance Schedule: Develop a regular maintenance schedule for HVAC systems, ensuring that all components related to humidity control are checked and serviced as needed.

4. Stay Informed on Best Practices: Keep abreast of best practices for humidity management by consulting HVAC professionals and reading industry publications.

In summary, controlling humidity is essential for maintaining health and comfort in indoor environments. By understanding the role of humidity, implementing effective HVAC solutions, and adopting best practices for humidity management, individuals can significantly enhance their quality of life. As we continue to explore the connection between HVAC systems and health, we will uncover additional factors that contribute to creating a healthier and more comfortable living environment.

Conclusion

As we reach the conclusion of this comprehensive exploration of HVAC (Heating, Ventilation, and Air Conditioning), it's imperative to reflect on the extensive knowledge and insights captured within these twelve volumes. This collection not only elucidates the foundational principles of HVAC systems but also delves into the advancements and complexities that define the modern landscape of this vital industry.

From the outset, we established a solid groundwork in HVAC fundamentals. The initial chapters defined key concepts, explored essential components, and traced the evolution of HVAC technology over the years. This foundational understanding is crucial for anyone navigating the intricate world of HVAC. Readers have gained valuable insights into how heating, cooling, and ventilation systems work together to create comfortable and efficient indoor environments. The historical context provided throughout highlights how innovations have shaped contemporary practices, underscoring the importance of adaptability and continual improvement in this field.

As we transitioned into detailed examinations of various HVAC components, the series provided an in-depth look at the specific functionalities of heating units, cooling systems, and ventilation strategies. Each component—whether it be a furnace, heat pump, or air conditioning unit—has been analyzed regarding its design, operational principles, and maintenance requirements. This comprehensive approach allows readers to appreciate how these systems function both independently and as integrated parts of larger HVAC frameworks, achieving optimal performance in real-world applications.

The chapters dedicated to installation techniques and maintenance practices serve as invaluable resources for both aspiring technicians and seasoned professionals. The hands-on guidance emphasizes the importance of meticulous planning and execution during installation, illustrating how proper setup directly influences system efficiency and longevity. Routine maintenance is equally critical, and the series outlines systematic procedures to ensure HVAC systems operate at peak performance. By incorporating troubleshooting techniques and practical advice, readers are equipped with the skills to identify and resolve common issues, ultimately enhancing reliability and reducing downtime.

A particularly exciting focus of this series is the exploration of advanced technologies reshaping the HVAC industry. As the demand for energy efficiency and sustainability grows, the integration of smart technologies and IoT (Internet of Things) applications within HVAC systems becomes increasingly prevalent. Readers have learned how smart thermostats, automated controls, and energy management systems are revolutionizing HVAC operations, empowering users to make data-driven decisions about energy consumption and comfort.

Moreover, we emphasized the critical connection between HVAC systems and health and wellness. The management of indoor air quality (IAQ) and humidity levels is vital for promoting a healthy living environment. Readers have gained insights into the strategies necessary for maintaining optimal indoor air quality, as well as the tools to effectively monitor and control humidity. This holistic understanding of HVAC management reinforces the systems' role in enhancing not only comfort but also overall well-being.

The examination of specialized HVAC applications revealed the unique requirements across various environments, including commercial, industrial, and healthcare settings. Each sector presents distinct challenges that necessitate tailored HVAC solutions. For instance, healthcare facilities often demand rigorous indoor air quality standards to safeguard patient health, while industrial environments may require systems capable of managing significant temperature fluctuations. Through detailed case studies and real-world examples, we illustrated how HVAC professionals successfully navigate these challenges, employing innovative solutions that enhance both efficiency and comfort.

Throughout this series, we have also underscored the significance of adhering to regulatory standards and best practices. Compliance with local and national building codes, safety regulations, and environmental guidelines is not merely a legal obligation; it is essential for ensuring the safety and efficacy of HVAC systems. The insights provided in this collection empower HVAC professionals to operate within legal frameworks while promoting ethical practices that benefit both clients and the environment.

In the ever-evolving realm of HVAC, the integration of smart home technologies represents a significant paradigm shift. The exploration of smart HVAC systems highlights the transformative potential of connectivity and automation in enhancing user comfort and energy efficiency. By utilizing smart thermostats, automated controls, and IoT applications, homeowners gain unprecedented control over their indoor environments. This integration not only allows for tailored temperature settings based on individual preferences but also facilitates real-time monitoring and management of energy consumption. As the trend towards smart homes continues to grow, HVAC professionals must remain adept at implementing these technologies, ensuring seamless integration that enhances the overall user experience while contributing to sustainability goals.

Moreover, the critical role of HVAC systems in promoting health and wellness cannot be overstated. The emphasis on indoor air quality (IAQ) and humidity control underscores the necessity of maintaining healthy environments that support physical and mental well-being. Readers have been equipped with strategies to effectively manage humidity levels, mitigate pollutants, and enhance ventilation—all crucial elements for fostering optimal indoor air quality. By prioritizing these aspects, HVAC professionals can significantly impact occupant health and comfort, ultimately leading to improved productivity and quality of life. This holistic approach to HVAC management emphasizes that beyond mere climate control, the industry has a profound responsibility to contribute positively to the health and wellness of individuals and communities alike.

As we look ahead, the concluding insights presented in this collection highlight the necessity for ongoing education and adaptation. The HVAC industry is in a perpetual state of evolution, propelled by technological advancements, regulatory shifts, and changing consumer expectations. For professionals in the field, staying informed and engaged with emerging trends and innovations is paramount. Whether through continued education, networking with industry peers, or participating in professional organizations, a commitment to lifelong learning is essential for success in this dynamic landscape.

In summary, this series serves as a comprehensive resource for understanding the vast and intricate world of HVAC systems. From foundational knowledge to advanced applications, each chapter contributes to a holistic understanding of the industry. Readers are equipped with not only technical expertise but also the contextual knowledge necessary to excel in a rapidly changing environment. The insights gained from this collection will undoubtedly serve as a valuable asset for anyone looking to enhance their knowledge, improve their skills, and navigate the complexities of HVAC systems with confidence.

As you embark on your HVAC journey, may the knowledge acquired from this series empower you to embrace challenges, foster innovation, and contribute to the continued advancement of this essential industry. Thank you for taking this educational journey with us; your commitment to mastering HVAC principles and practices is vital for creating comfortable, efficient, and healthy indoor environments for all.

Made in United States
Troutdale, OR
02/28/2025